1001
COCKTAILS
IN A SHAKE

The Home Bartender's Guide

By William C. Kuney

© COPYRIGHT 1976 AND PUBLISHED BY
COLES PUBLISHING COMPANY LIMITED
TORONTO—CANADA

PRINTED IN CANADA

INDEX

5

INDEX

INDEX

INDEX

COCKTAILS
With Curacao

COCKTAILS
With Dry Gin

INDEX

9

INDEX

COCKTAILS
With Dubonnet

COCKTAILS
With Kummel

COCKTAILS
With Nectar Liqueur

COCKTAILS
With
Orange Flavored Gin

COCKTAILS
With Rum

INDEX

INDEX

COCKTAILS
With Vodka

COCKTAILS
With Whiskey
(Bourbon or Rye)

COCKTAILS
With Whiskey
(Irish)

COCKTAILS
With Whiskey
(Scotch)

COCKTAILS
With Wine
(Claret, Madeira, Muscatel, Sherry, White)

INDEX

13

INDEX

14

15

ABBEY COCKTAIL

1½ oz. Dry Gin
Juice of ¼ Orange
1 Dash Orange Bitters
Shake well with cracked Ice and strain into 3 oz. Cocktail glass. Add a Maraschino Cherry.

ABSINTHE COCKTAIL

1½ oz. Absinthe Substitute
¾ oz. Water
¼ oz. Anisette
1 Dash Orange Bitters
Shake well with cracked Ice and strain into 3 oz. Cocktail glass.

ABSINTHE DRIP COCKTAIL

1½ oz. Absinthe Substitute
Dissolve 1 lump of Sugar, using the French drip spoon, and fill glass with cold water. Use Old Fashioned Cocktail glass.

ABSINTHE SPECIAL COCKTAIL

1½ oz. Absinthe Substitute
1 oz. Water
¼ Teaspoon Powdered Sugar
1 Dash Orange Bitters
Shake well with cracked Ice and strain into 3 oz. Cocktail glass.

ADONIS COCKTAIL

1 Dash Orange Bitters
¾ oz. Italian Vermouth
1½ oz. Dry Sherry
Stir well with cracked Ice and strain into 3 oz. Cocktail glass.

AFFINITY COCKTAIL

¾ oz. French Vermouth
¾ oz. Italian Vermouth
¾ oz. Scotch Whiskey
2 Dashes Orange Bitters
Stir well with cracked Ice and strain into 3 oz. Cocktail glass.

1 oz. Apricot Flavored Brandy
1 oz. Curacao
½ Teaspoon Lemon Juice
Shake well with cracked Ice and strain
into 3 oz. Cocktail glass.

AFTER DINNER COCKTAIL

1 oz. Apricot Flavored Brandy
1 oz. Curacao
½ oz. Lemon Juice
Shake well with cracked Ice and strain
into 3 oz. Cocktail glass.

AFTER SUPPER COCKTAIL

½ oz. Lemon Juice
½ Teaspoon Powdered Sugar
1½ oz. Brandy
1 Teaspoon Curacao
Shake well with cracked Ice and strain
into 3 oz. Cocktail glass.

ALABAMA COCKTAIL

Juice ½ Lemon
1 Teaspoon Powdered Sugar
2 oz. Dry Gin
Shake well with cracked Ice and strain
into 7 oz. Highball glass. Fill with
Carbonated Water. Add 2 Sprigs of
Fresh Mint.

ALABAMA FIZZ

2 Dashes Orange Bitters
1½ oz. Dry Gin
¾ oz. Yellow Chartreuse
Stir well with cracked Ice and strain
into 3 oz. Cocktail glass.

ALASKA COCKTAIL

Juice ½ Lemon
1 Teaspoon Powdered Sugar
2 oz. Dry Gin
Shake well with cracked Ice and strain
into 7 oz. Highball glass. Fill with
Carbonated Water. Add 1 Teaspoon
Raspberry Syrup.

ALBEMARLE FIZZ

ALEXANDER COCKTAIL No. 1

1 oz. Dry Gin
1 oz. Creme de Cacao
1 oz. Sweet Cream
Shake well and with cracked Ice and strain into 4 oz. Cocktail glass.

ALEXANDER COCKTAIL No. 2

1 oz. Creme de Cacao
1 oz. Brandy
1 oz. Sweet Cream
Shake well with cracked Ice and strain into 4 oz. Cocktail glass.

ALEXANDER'S SISTER COCKTAIL

1 oz. Dry Gin
1 oz. Creme de Menthe
1 oz. Sweet Cream
Shake well with cracked Ice and strain into 4 oz. Cocktail glass.

ALLEN COCKTAIL

¼ oz. Lemon Juice
¾ oz. Maraschino
1 ½ oz. Dry Gin
Shake well with cracked Ice and strain into 3 oz. Cocktail glass.

ALLIES COCKTAIL

1 oz. French Vermouth
1 oz. Dry Gin
½ Teaspoon Kummel
Shake well with cracked Ice and strain into 3 oz. Cocktail glass.

AMER PICON COCKTAIL

Juice 1 Lime
1 Teaspoon Grenadine
1½ oz. Amer Picon
Shake well with cracked Ice and strain into 3 oz. Cocktail glass.

½ oz. Orange Juice
½ oz. Grenadine
½ oz. French Vermouth
½ oz. Brandy
¼ Teaspoon Creme de Menthe
Shake well with cracked Ice and strain
into 3 oz. Cocktail glass and top with a
little Port Wine.

**AMERICAN
BEAUTY
COCKTAIL**

1 Lump of Sugar
Juice ¼ Lemon
1½ oz. Imported Rum
Fill Hot Whiskey glass with hot Water
and stir.

AMERICAN GROG

¼ oz. Grenadine
¼ oz. Triple Sec
¼ oz. Creme Yvette
¼ oz. Fresh Cream
Pour carefully, in order given, into
Pousse Cafe glass, so that each
ingredient floats on preceding one.

ANGEL'S DELIGHT

¼ oz. Creme de Cacao
¼ oz. Creme de Yvette
¼ oz. Brandy
¼ oz. Sweet Cream
Pour ingredients carefully, in order
given, so that they do not mix. Use
Pousse Cafe glass.

ANGEL'S KISS

¾ oz. Creme de Cacao
¼ oz. Sweet Cream
Float cream and insert toothpick in
Cherry and put on top. Use Pousse
Cafe glass.

ANGEL'S TIP

19

ANGEL'S WING

$\frac{1}{3}$ oz. Creme de Cacao
$\frac{1}{3}$ oz. Brandy
$\frac{1}{3}$ oz. Sweet Cream
Pour ingredients carefully, in order given, so that they do not mix. Use Pousse Cafe glass.

APPARENT COCKTAIL

1 oz. Dry Gin
1 oz. Creme de Cacao
$\frac{1}{4}$ Teaspoon Absinthe substitute
Shake well with cracked Ice and strain into 3 oz. Cocktail glass.

APPETIZER COCKTAIL

$\frac{3}{4}$ oz. Dry Gin
$\frac{3}{4}$ oz. Dubonnet
Juice of $\frac{1}{4}$ Orange
Shake well with cracked Ice and strain into 3 oz. Cocktail glass.

APPLE BLOW FIZZ

White of 1 Egg
Juice $\frac{1}{2}$ Lemon
1 Teaspoon Powdered Sugar
2 oz. Applejack
Shake well with cracked Ice and strain into 8 oz. Highball glass. Fill with Carbonated Water.

APPLEJACK COCKTAIL

$1\frac{1}{2}$ oz. Applejack
1 Teaspoon Grenadine
1 Teaspoon Lemon Juice
Shake well with cracked Ice and strain into 3 oz. Cocktail glass.

APPLEJACK HIGHBALL

1 Cube of ice
2 oz. Applejack
Fill 8 oz. Highball glass with Ginger Ale or Carbonated Water. Add Twist of Lemon Peel, if desired, and stir gently.

1 Cube of ice
  Juice of ½ Lime
1½ oz. Applejack
Fill 8 oz. Highball glass with
Carbonated Water and stir. Leave
Lime in glass.

APPLEJACK RICKEY

Juice ½ Lemon
½ Teaspoon Powdered Sugar
2 oz. Applejack
Shake well with cracked Ice and strain
into 6 oz. Sour glass. Fill with
Carbonated Water. Decorate with a
slice of Lemon and a Cherry.

APPLEJACK SOUR

¾ oz. Imported Rum
¾ oz. Italian Vermouth
1 Teaspoon Apricot Flavored Brandy
½ Teaspoon Grenadine
1 Teaspoon Lemon Juice
Shake well with cracked Ice and strain
into 3 oz. Cocktail glass.

APPLE PIE COCKTAIL

1½ oz. Rye or Bourbon Whiskey
2 Dashes Bitters
½ Teaspoon Curacao
Twist of Orange and Lemon Peel. Stir
well with cracked Ice and strain into 3
oz. Cocktail glass.

APPROVE COCKTAIL

Juice of ¼ Lemon
Juice of ¼ Orange
1½ oz. Apricot Flavored Brandy
1 Teaspoon Dry Gin
Shake well with cracked Ice and strain
into 3 oz. Cocktail glass.

APRICOT COCKTAIL

APPRICOT COOLER

Into 12 oz. Tom Collins glass, put:
1/2 Teaspoon Powdered Sugar
2 oz. Carbonated Water, and stir.
Fill glass with Cracked Ice and add:
2 oz. Apricot Flavored Brandy.
Fill with Carbonated Water or Ginger Ale.
Insert spiral of Orange or Lemon Peel (or both) and dangle end over rim of glass.

APRICOT FIZZ

Juice 1/2 Lemon
Juice 1/2 Lime
1 Teaspoon Powdered Sugar
2 oz. Apricot Flavored Brandy
Shake well with cracked Ice and strain into 7 oz. Highball glass. Fill with Carbonated Water.

APRICOT NECTAR RICKEY

1 Cube of Ice
Juice of 1/2 Lime
2 oz. Apricot Nectar
Fill 8 oz. Highball glass with Carbonated Water and stir. Leave Lime in glass.

AROUND THE WORLD COCKTAIL

1 oz. Pineapple Juice
1/2 oz. Green Creme de Menthe
1/2 oz. Dry Gin
Shake well with cracked Ice and strain into 3 oz. Cocktail glass.

ATTY COCKTAIL

1/2 oz. French Vermouth
1 1/2 oz. Dry Gin
1/2 Teaspoon Creme de Yvette
Shake well with cracked Ice and strain into 3 oz. Cocktail glass.

½ oz. Benedictine
½ oz. Cognac
Use Cordial glass and carefully float
the Cognac on top of the Benedictine.

B & B

½ oz. Sweet Cream
1½ oz. Apricot Flavored Brandy
¼ Teaspoon Dry Gin
Shake well with cracked Ice and strain
into 3 oz. Cocktail glass.

**BABBIE'S SPECIAL
COCKTAIL**

1½ oz. Bacardi Rum
Juice ½ Lime
½ Teaspoon Grenadine
Shake well with cracked Ice and strain
into 3 oz. Cocktail glass.

**BACARDI
COCKTAIL**

1½ oz. Dry Gin
White of 1 Egg
1 Dash Orange Bitters
½ Teaspoon Grenadine
Shake well with cracked Ice and strain
into 4 oz. Cocktail glass.

**BACHELOR'S BAIT
COCKTAIL**

1 oz. Anisette
1 oz. Brandy
White of 1 Egg
Shake well with cracked Ice and strain
into 4 oz. Cocktail glass.

**BALTIMORE
BRACER COCKTAIL**

1 Egg
1 Teaspoon Powdered Sugar
½ oz. Apricot Flavored Brandy
½ oz. Imported Rum
1 oz. Madeira Wine
Fill glass with Milk, shake well with
cracked Ice and strain into 12 oz. Tom
Collins glass. Grate Nutmeg on top.

**BALTIMORE
EGG NOG**

BAMBOO COCKTAIL

1½ oz. Sherry
¾ oz. French Vermouth
1 Dash Orange Bitters
Stir well with cracked Ice and strain into 3 oz. Cocktail glass.

BARBARY COAST COCKTAIL

½ oz. Dry Gin
½ oz. Imported Rum
½ oz. Creme de Cacao
½ oz. Scotch Whiskey
½ oz. Sweet Cream
Shake well with cracked Ice and strain into 4 oz. Cocktail glass.

BARON COCKTAIL

½ oz. French Vermouth
1½ oz. Dry Gin
1½ Teaspoons Curacao
½ Teaspoon Italian Vermouth
Stir well with cracked Ice and strain into 3 oz. Cocktail glass. Add twist of Lemon Peel and drop in glass.

BARTON SPECIAL COCKTAIL

½ oz. Apple Brandy
½ oz. Scotch Whiskey
1½ oz. Dry Gin
Stir well with cracked Ice and strain into 3 oz. Cocktail glass.

BEADLESTONE COCKTAIL

1¼ oz. French Vermouth
1¼ oz. Scotch Whiskey
Stir well with cracked Ice and strain into 3 oz. Cocktail glass.

BEALS COCKTAIL

1½ oz. Scotch Whiskey
½ oz. French Vermouth
½ oz. Italian Vermouth
Stir well with cracked Ice and strain into 3 oz. Cocktail glass.

24

1 Teaspoon Orange Juice
½ oz. Italian Vermouth
½ oz. French Vermouth
1 oz. Dry Gin
Shake well with cracked Ice and strain
into 3 oz. Cocktail glass, with a Dash of
Grenadine in bottom of glass.

**BEAUTY SPOT
COCKTAIL**

2 oz. Dry Gin
1 Teaspoon Raspberry Syrup
¾ oz. Sweet Cream
Shake well with cracked Ice and strain
into 4 oz. Cocktail glass.

**BELMONT
COCKTAIL**

Juice of ½ Lime
1½ oz. Dry Gin
½ Teaspoon Powdered Sugar
2 Dashes Orange Bitters
Shake well with cracked Ice and strain
into 3 oz. Cocktail glass.

**BENNETT
COCKTAIL**

Juice ¼ Orange
Juice ½ Lemon
1 Teaspoon Powdered Sugar
1½ oz. Dry Gin
1 oz. Apricot Flavored Brandy
1 Teaspoon Grenadine
½ Teaspoon Curacao
Shake well with cracked Ice and strain
into 8 oz. Highball glass.

**BERMUDA
BOUQUET**

1 Cube of Ice
¾ oz. Dry Gin
¾ oz. Brandy
¾ oz. French Vermouth
Fill 8 oz. Highball glass with Ginger
Ale or Carbonated Water. Add Twist
of Lemon Peel, if desired, and stir
gently.

**BERMUDA
HIGHBALL**

BERMUDA ROSE COCKTAIL

1¼ oz. Dry Gin
¼ oz. Apricot Nectar Liqueur
¼ oz. Grenadine
Shake well with cracked Ice and strain into 3 oz. Cocktail glass.

BETWEEN THE SHEETS COCKTAIL

Juice ¼ Lemon
½ oz. Brandy
½ oz. Triple Sec
½ oz. Imported Rum
Shake well with cracked Ice and strain into 3 oz. Cocktail glass.

BIFFY COCKTAIL

Juice of ½ Lemon
½ oz. Swedish Punch
1½ oz. Dry Gin
Shake well with cracked Ice and strain into 3 oz. Cocktail glass.

BIJOU COCKTAIL

¾ oz. Dry Gin
¾ oz. Green Chartreuse
¾ oz. Italian Vermouth
1 Dash Orange Bitters
Shake well with cracked Ice and strain into 3 oz. Cocktail glass. Add Cherry on top.

BILLY TAYLOR

Juice ½ Lime
2 Cubes of Ice
2 oz. Dry Gin
Fill 12 oz. Tom Collins glass with Carbonated Water and stir gently.

BIRD OF PARADISE FIZZ

Juice ½ Lemon
1 Teaspoon Powdered Sugar
White of 1 egg
1 Teaspoon Grenadine
2 oz. Dry Gin
Shake well with cracked Ice and strain into 8 oz. Highball glass. Fill with Carbonated Water.

Juice ¼ Lemon
Juice ¼ Orange
1 Teaspoon Powdered Sugar
Pour into 8 oz. Highball glass. Add
cube of Ice, fill with Burgundy and stir
well. Decorate with Fruits.

BISHOP

1 Cube of Ice
¾ oz. Bitters
Fill 8 oz. Highball glass with Ginger
Ale or Carbonated Water. Add twist
of Lemon Peel, if desired, and stir
gently.

**BITTERS
HIGHBALL**

1¼ oz. Rye or Bourbon Whiskey
1¼ oz. Sloe Gin
Stir well with cracked Ice and strain
into 3 oz. Cocktail glass. Serve with a
Cherry.

**BLACK HAWK
COCKTAIL**

2 oz. Imported Rum
1 Tablespoon Molasses
Shake well with cracked Ice and strain
into 3 oz. Cocktail glass.

**BLACK STRIPE
COCKTAIL**

1½ oz. Sloe Gin
¾ oz. French Vermouth
1 Dash Orange Bitters
Shake well with cracked Ice and strain
into 3 oz. Cocktail glass. Serve with a
Slice of Lemon.

**BLACKTHORN
COCKTAIL**

5 oz. Stout
5 oz. Champagne
Pour very carefully into 12 oz. Glass
with cubes of Ice and stir very gently.

BLACK VELVET

BLARNEY STONE COCKTAIL

2 oz. Irish Whiskey
½ Teaspoon Absinthe Substitute
½ Teaspoon Curacao
¼ Teaspoon Maraschino
1 Dash Bitters
Shake well with cracked Ice and strain into 3 oz. Cocktail glass. Twist of Orange Peel and serve with an Olive.

BLENTON COCKTAIL

¾ oz. French Vermouth
1½ oz. Dry Gin
1 Dash Orange Bitters.
Stir well with cracked Ice and strain into 3 oz. Cocktail glass. Add a Cherry.

BLOCK AND FALL COCKTAIL

¼ oz. Anisette
¼ oz. Applejack
¾ oz. Brandy
¾ oz. Triple Sec
Shake well with cracked Ice and strain into 3 oz. Cocktail glass.

BLOOD AND SAND COCKTAIL

½ oz. Orange Juice
½ oz. Scotch Whiskey
½ oz. Wild Cherry Flavored Brandy
½ oz. Italian Vermouth
Shake well with cracked Ice and strain into 3 oz. Cocktail glass.

BLOOD BRONX COCKTAIL

1½ oz. Dry Gin
¼ oz. French Vermouth
Juice of ¼ Blood Orange
Shake well with cracked Ice and strain into 3 oz. Cocktail glass.

BLOODHOUND COCKTAIL

½ oz. French Vermouth
½ oz. Italian Vermouth
1 oz. Dry Gin
2 or 3 crushed Strawberries
Shake well with cracked Ice and strain into 3 oz. Cocktail glass.

BLUE BLAZER

Use two large silver-plated mugs, with handles.
2½ oz. Bourbon Whiskey
2½ oz. Boiling Water
Put the whiskey into one mug, and the boiling water into the other, ignite the whiskey and, while blazing, mix both ingredients by pouring them four or five times from one mug to the other. If well done, this will have the appearance of a continued stream of liquid fire.
Sweeten with 1 teaspoon of Powdered Sugar and serve with a piece of Lemon . Peel. Serve in 4 oz. Hot Whiskey glass.

BLUE DEVIL COCKTAIL

1 oz. Dry Gin
   Juice ½ Lemon or 1 Lime
½ oz. Maraschino
½ Teaspoon Creme de Yvette
Shake well with cracked Ice and strain into 3 oz. Cocktail glass.

BLUE MOON COCKTAIL

1½ oz. Dry Gin
   ¾ oz. Creme de Yvette
Shake well with cracked Ice and strain into 3 oz. Cocktail glass. Add twist of Lemon Peel and drop in glass.

BOBBY BURNS COCKTAIL

1¼ oz. Italian Vermouth
1¼ oz. Scotch Whiskey
   1 Teaspoon Benedictine
Stir well with cracked Ice and strain into 3 oz. Cocktail glass. Add twist of Lemon Peel and drop in glass.

BOLERO COCKTAIL

1½ oz. Imported Rum.
   ¾ oz. Applejack
   ¼ Teaspoon Italian Vermouth
Shake well with cracked Ice and strain into 3 oz. Cocktail glass.

BOLO COCKTAIL

2 oz. Imported Rum
Juice of ½ Lime
Juice of ¼ Orange
1 Tablespoon Powdered Sugar
Stir well with cracked Ice and strain into 4 oz. Cocktail glass.

BOMBAY COCKTAIL

½ oz. French Vermouth
½ oz. Italian Vermouth
1 oz. Brandy
¼ Teaspoon Absinthe substitute
½ Teaspoon Curacao
Shake well with cracked Ice and strain into 3 oz. Cocktail glass.

BOMBAY PUNCH

Juice of 1 Dozen Lemons
Add enough Powdered Sugar to Sweeten
Place large block of Ice in Punch bowl and stir. Then add:
1 qt. Brandy
1 qt. Sherry Wine
¼ pt. Maraschino
¼ pt. Curacao
4 qts. Champagne
2 qts. Carbonated Water
Some prefer to add the strained contents of a Pot of Tea. Stir well and decorate with fruits in season. Serve in 4 oz. Punch glasses.

BOOSTER COCKTAIL

1 Teaspoon Curacao
White of 1 Egg
2 oz. Brandy
Shake well with cracked Ice and strain into 4 oz. Cocktail glass. Grate Nutmeg on top.

¾ oz. Dry Gin
¾ oz. Apricot Nectar Liqueur
    Juice of ¼ Lemon
¼ oz. Grenadine
Stir well with cracked Ice and strain
into 3 oz. Cocktail glass.

**BOSTON
COCKTAIL**

Into 12 oz. Tom Collins glass, put:
    Juice ½ Lemon
1 Teaspoon Powdered Sugar
2 oz. Carbonated Water, and stir.
    Fill glass with Cracked Ice and add:
2 oz. Imported Rum
    Fill with Carbonated Water or
    Ginger Ale
Insert spiral of Orange or Lemon Peel
(or both) and dangle end over rim of
glass.

BOSTON COOLER

¾ oz. Brandy
¾ oz. Imported Rum
¾ oz. Triple Sec
    Juice ½ Lime
Shake well with cracked Ice and strain
into 3 oz. Cocktail glass.

**BOSTON SIDE
CAR COCKTAIL**

    Juice ½ Lemon
1 Teaspoon Powdered Sugar
2 oz. Rye or Bourbon Whiskey
    White of 1 Egg
Shake well with cracked Ice and strain
into 8 oz. Highball glass. Then add
piece of Ice, fill with Carbonated
Water and decorate with half-slice of
Lemon and a Cherry.

BOSTON SOUR

BOURBON **HIGHBALL**	1 Cube of Ice 2 oz. Bourbon Whiskey Fill 8 oz. Highball glass with Ginger Ale or Carbonated Water. Add twist of Lemon Peel, if desired, and stir gently.
BRAINSTORM **COCKTAIL**	Cube of Ice ½ Teaspoon Benedictine 1 Piece Orange Peel ½ Teaspoon French Vermouth 2 oz. Irish Whiskey Serve with a small bar spoon. Use Old Fashioned Cocktail glass and stir.
BRANDY AND **SODA**	2 Cubes of Ice 2 oz. Brandy 6 oz. Carbonated Water Service in 12 oz. Tom Collins glass and stir.
BRANDY BLAZER	1 Lump Sugar 1 Piece Orange Peel 1 Piece Lemon Peel 2 oz. Brandy Use Old Fashioned Cocktail glass. Light with a match, stir with long spoon for a few seconds and strain into a Hot Whiskey glass.
BRANDY COBBLER	1 Teaspoon Powdered Sugar 2 oz. Carbonated Water Fill 10 oz. Goblet with Shaved Ice Add 2 oz. Brandy Stir well and decorate with fruits in season. Serve with straws.

2 oz. Brandy
¼ Teaspoon Simple Syrup
2 Dashes Bitters
  Twist of Lemon Peel
Stir well with cracked Ice and strain
into 3 oz. Cocktail glass.

BRANDY COCKTAIL

  Juice ½ Lemon
1 Teaspoon Powdered Sugar
2 oz. Brandy
Pour into 12 oz. Tom Collins glass. Add
several Cubes of Ice, fill with
Carbonated Water and stir well.
Decorate with slice of Orange, Lemon
and a Cherry, Serve with straws.

BRANDY COLLINS

Moisten the edge of 4 oz. Cocktail glass
with Lemon and dip into Sugar. Cut
the rind of half a Lemon in a spiral, and
place in glass.
1 Teaspoon Maraschino
1 Dash Bitters
1 Teaspoon Lemon Juice
½ oz. Curacao
2 oz. Brandy
Stir above ingredients in mixing glass
and strain into glass prepared as
above. Add Slice of Orange.

BRANDY CRUSTA COCKTAIL

  Juice of ½ Lemon
½ Teaspoon Powdered Sugar
1 Teaspoon Raspberry Syrup or
  Grenadine
2 oz. Brandy
Shake well with cracked Ice and strain
into Stein or 8 oz. metal cup. Add Cube
of Ice and decorate with fruit.

BRANDY DAISY

33

BRANDY EGG NOG

1 Egg
1 Teaspoon Powdered Sugar
2 oz. Brandy
  Fill glass with Milk
Shake well with cracked Ice and strain into 12 oz. Tom Collins glass. Grate Nutmeg on top.

BRANDY FIX

  Juice ½ Lemon
1 Teaspoon Powdered Sugar
1 Teaspoon Water and stir
  Fill glass with Shaved Ice
2 oz. Brandy
½ oz. Wild Cherry Flavored Brandy
Use 12 oz. Tom Collins glass. Stir well. Add slice of Lemon. Serve with straws.

BRANDY FIZZ

  Juice ½ Lemon
1 Teaspoon Powdered Sugar
2 oz. Brandy
Shake well with cracked Ice and strain into 7 oz. Highball glass. Fill with Carbonated Water.

BRANDY FLIP

  1 Egg
  1 Teaspoon Powdered Sugar
1½ oz. Brandy
  2 Teaspoons Sweet Cream
    (if desired)
Shake well with cracked Ice and strain into 5 oz. Flip glass. Grate a little Nutmeg on top.

BRANDY GUMP COCKTAIL

1½ oz. Brandy
  Juice of ½ Lemon
½ Teaspoon Grenadine
Shake well with cracked Ice and strain into 3 oz. Cocktail glass.

1 Cube of Ice
2 oz. Brandy
Fill 8 oz. Highball glass with Ginger
Ale or Carbonated Water. Add twist
of Lemon Peel, if desired, and stir
gently.

BRANDY HIGHBALL

Into 12 oz. Tom Collins glass put:
1 Teaspoon Powdered Sugar
5 or 6 Sprigs Fresh Mint
2 oz. Brandy
1 oz. Peach Flavored Brandy
Then fill glass with finely shaved Ice,
and stir until Mint rises to top, being
careful not to bruise Mint. (Do not hold
glass with hand while stirring.)
Decorate with slice of Pineapple,
Orange, Lemon and a Cherry. Serve
with straws.

BRANDY JULEP

1 Teaspoon Powdered Sugar
2 oz. Brandy
½ Pint Milk
Shake well with cracked Ice, strain
into 12 oz. Tom Collins glass and grate
Nutmeg on top.

BRANDY MILK PUNCH

Juice of 1 Dozen Lemons
Juice of 4 Oranges
Add enough Sugar to sweeten
8 oz. Grenadine
1 qt. Carbonated Water
Place large block of Ice in Punch
Bowl and stir well. Then add:
½ Pint Curacao
2 qts. Brandy
Some prefer to add the strained
contents of a Pot of Tea. Stir well and
decorate with fruits in season. Serve
in 4 oz. Punch glasses.

BRANDY PUNCH

BRANDY SANGAREE

1½ oz. Brandy
1 Teaspoon Powdered Sugar
Shake well with cracked Ice and strain into 3 oz. Cocktail glass, leaving enough room in which to float a Tablespoon of Port Wine.

BRANDY SLING

Dissolve 1 Teaspoon Powdered Sugar in Teaspoon of Water.
2 oz. Brandy
2 Cubes of Ice
Serve in Old Fashioned Cocktail glass and stir. Twist of Lemon Peel and drop in glass.

BRANDY SMASH

Muddle 1 Lump of Sugar with
1 oz. Carbonated Water and
4 Sprigs of Green Mint
Add 2 oz. Brandy, then a Cube of Ice. Stir and decorate with a slice of Orange and a Cherry. Twist Lemon Peel on top. Use Old Fashioned Cocktail glass.

BRANDY SOUR

Juice ½ Lemon
½ Teaspoon Powdered Sugar
2 oz. Brandy
Shake well with cracked Ice and strain into 6 oz. Sour glass. Fill with Carbonated Water. Decorate with a half-slice of Lemon and a Cherry.

BRANDY SQUIRT

1½ oz. Brandy
1 Tablespoon Powdered Sugar
1 Teaspoon Raspberry Syrup or Grenadine.
Stir well with cracked Ice and strain into 8 oz. Highball glass and fill with Carbonated Water. Decorate with Cubes of Pineapple and Strawberries.

Made same as Gin Swizzle, using 2 oz. Brandy.

BRANDY SWIZZLE

Use Old Fashioned Cocktail glass.
½ Teaspoon Powdered Sugar
2 Teaspoons Water
2 oz. Brandy
1 Lump of Ice
Stir well and Twist Lemon Peel on top.

BRANDY TODDY

Put lump of Sugar into Hot Whiskey glass and fill with two-thirds Boiling Water. Add 2 oz. Brandy. Stir and decorate with Slice of Lemon. Grate Nutmeg on top.

BRANDY TODDY
(Hot)

½ oz. Italian Vermouth
2 oz. Brandy
1 Dash Bitters
Stir well with cracked Ice and strain into 3 oz. Cocktail glass.

BRANDY VERMOUTH COCKTAIL

1¼ oz. French Vermouth
1¼ oz. Sherry Wine
1 Dash Bitters
¼ Teaspoon Absinthe substitute
Stir well with cracked Ice and strain into 3 oz. Cocktail glass.

BRAZIL COCKTAIL

1 Egg
½ oz. Curacao
2 oz. Apricot Flavored Brandy
Fill glass with Milk
Shake well with cracked Ice and strain into 12 oz. Tom Collins glass. Grate Nutmeg on top.

BREAKFAST EGG NOG

37

BRIGHTON PUNCH

¾ oz. Rye or Bourbon Whiskey
¾ oz. Cognac
¾ oz. Benedictine
Juice ½ Orange
Juice ½ Lemon
Fill 12 oz. Tom Collins glass with shaved Ice and Carbonated Water and stir. Serve with straws.

BROKEN SPUR COCKTAIL

¾ oz. Italian Vermouth
1½ oz. Port Wine
¼ Teaspoon Curacao
Shake well with cracked Ice and strain into 3 oz. Cocktail glass.

BRONX COCKTAIL

1 oz. Dry Gin
½ oz. French Vermouth
½ oz. Italian Vermouth
Juice ¼ Orange
Shake well with cracked Ice and strain into 3 oz. Cocktail glass. Serve with Slice of Orange

BRONX COCKTAIL [Dry]

1 oz. Dry Gin
1 oz. French Vermouth
Juice ¼ Orange
Shake well with cracked Ice and strain into 3 oz. Cocktail glass. Serve with Slice of Orange.

BRONX GOLDEN COCKTAIL

Made same as Bronx Cocktail, adding the Yolk of one Egg. Use 4 oz. Cocktail glass.

BRONX SILVER COCKTAIL

Juice of ¼ Orange
White of 1 Egg
½ oz. French Vermouth
1 oz. Dry Gin
Shake well with cracked Ice and strain into 4 oz. Cocktail glass.

1½ oz. Dry Gin
1½ oz. French Vermouth
   Juice of ½ Lime
Shake well with cracked Ice and strain
into 3 oz. Cocktail glass. Add a Cherry.

BRONX TERRACE COCKTAIL

¾ oz. Dry Gin
¾ oz. Imported Rum
¾ oz. French Vermouth
Stir well with cracked Ice and strain
into 3 oz. Cocktail glass.

BROWN COCKTAIL

1 oz. Absinthe Substitute
1 Teaspoon Powdered Sugar
   Juice ½ Lemon
Shake well with cracked Ice and strain
into 3 oz. Cocktail glass.

BRUNELLE COCKTAIL

¼ Glass Orange Juice
   Fill with Champagne
Use 12 oz. Tom Collins glass

BUCKS FIZZ

1¼ oz. Wild Cherry Nectar Liqueur
¾ oz. Dry Gin
   Juice of ½ Lime
Shake well with cracked Ice and strain
into 3 oz. Cocktail glass.

BULLDOG COCKTAIL

1 Cube of Ice
   Juice of ½ Orange
2 oz. Dry Gin
Fill 8 oz. Highball glass with Ginger
Ale and stir.

BULLDOG HIGHBALL

1 oz. Brandy
2 oz. Hard Cider
1 Cube of Ice
Fill 8 oz. Highball glass with Ginger
Ale and stir.

BULL'S EYE

BULL'S MILK	1 Teaspoon Powdered Sugar
	1 oz. Imported Rum
	1½ oz. Brandy
	½ pt. Milk
	Shake well with cracked Ice and strain into 12 oz. Tom Collins glass. Grate Nutmeg and pinch of Cinnamon on top.

BURGUNDY BISHOP	Juice ¼ Lemon
	1 Teaspoon Powdered Sugar
	1 oz. Imported Rum
	Shake well and strain into 8 oz. Highball glass and fill with Burgundy and stir. Decorate with Fruits.

BUTTON HOOK COCKTAIL	½ oz. Creme de Menthe (White)
	½ oz. Apricot Flavored Brandy
	½ oz. Brandy
	½ oz. Absinthe Substitute
	Shake well with cracked Ice and strain into 3 oz. Cocktail glass.

B. V. D. COCKTAIL	¾ oz. French Vermouth
	¾ oz. Dry Gin
	¾ oz. Imported Rum
	Stir well with cracked ice and strain into 3 oz. Cocktail glass.

CARBARET COCKTAIL	1½ oz. Dry Gin
	2 Dashes Bitters
	½ Teaspoon French Vermouth
	¼ Teaspoon Benedictine
	Stir well with cracked Ice and strain into 3 oz. Cocktail glass. Serve with a Cherry.

Juice ½ Lemon
1 Teaspoon Powdered Sugar
2 oz. Rye or Bourbon Whiskey
Stir well with cracked Ice and fill with
Ginger Ale. Use 8 oz. Highball glass.

White of 1 Egg
1 Teaspoon Absinthe Substitute
1 Teaspoon Sweet Cream
1½ oz. Dry Gin
Shake well with cracked Ice and strain
into 4 oz. Cocktail glass.

1 Cup Hot Black Coffee
Put Cube of Sugar, well soaked with
Brandy, in teaspoon and hold so that it
will rest on top of coffee and ignite and
hold until flame burns out. Drop
contents in Coffee.

Juice 1 Lemon
Juice 1 Lime
3 Teaspoons Powdered Sugar
2 oz. Rye or Bourbon Whiskey
¼ Teaspoon Grenadine
Shake well with cracked Ice and strain
into 12 oz. Tom Collins glass filled with
Shaved Ice. Fill with Carbonated
Water and decorate with slice of
Orange, Lemon and a Cherry. Serve
with straws.

¾ oz. Scotch Whiskey
¾ oz. Irish Whiskey
Juice ¼ Lemon
2 Dashes Orange Bitters
Shake well with cracked Ice and strain
into 3 oz. Cocktail glass.

41

CARDINAL PUNCH

Juice of 1 Dozen Lemons
Add enough Powdered Sugar to
sweeten
1 qt Carbonated Water
Place large block of Ice in Punch
Bowl and stir well. Then add:
2 qts. Claret
1 pt. Brandy
1 pt. Imported Rum
1 pt. Champagne
½ pt. Italian Vermouth
Some prefer to add the strained
contents of a Pot of Tea. Stir well and
decorate with fruits in season. Serve
in 4 oz. Punch glasses.

CARROL COCKTAIL

1½ oz. Brandy
¾ oz. Italian Vermouth
Stir well with cracked Ice and strain
into 3 oz. Cocktail glass. Serve with a
Cherry.

CARUSO COCKTAIL

¾ oz. Dry Gin
¾ oz. French Vermouth
¾ oz. Creme de Menthe
(Green)
Stir well with cracked Ice and strain
into 3 oz. Cocktail glass.

CASCADE

1 oz. French Vermouth
1 oz. Creme de Cassis
1 Cube of Ice
Use 8 oz. Stem Goblet and fill balance
with Carbonated Water and stir.

CASINO COCKTAIL

2 Dashes Orange Bitters
¼ Teaspoon Maraschino
¼ Teaspoon Lemon Juice
2 oz. Dry Gin
Shake well with cracked Ice and strain
into 3 oz. Cocktail glass. Serve with a
Cherry.

1 oz. Apple Brandy
1 oz. Creme de Menthe (White)
½ Teaspoon Absinthe Substitute
Shake well with cracked Ice and strain
into 3 oz. Cocktail glass.

CASTLE DIP
COCKTAIL

Spiral Rind of ½ Lemon
1 Lump Sugar
2 Dashes Bitters
Fill with Champagne. Use 6 oz.
Champagne glass.

CHAMPAGNE
COCKTAIL

Use Large Glass Pitcher
4 Teaspoons Powdered Sugar
6 oz. Carbonated Water
½ oz. Triple Sec
½ oz. Curacao
2 oz. Brandy
Fill pitcher with cubes of Ice. Add 1
Pint of Champagne. Stir well and
decorate with as many fruits as
available and also Rind of Cucumber
inserted on each side of pitcher. Top
with small bunch of Mint Sprigs.
Serve in 5 oz. Claret glass.

CHAMPAGNE CUP

Juice of 1 Dozen Lemons
Add enough Powdered Sugar to
sweeten
1 qt. Carbonated Water.
Place large block of Ice in Punch
Bowl and stir well. Then add:
½ pt. Maraschino
½ pt. Curacao
1 pt. Brandy
2 qts. Champagne
Some prefer to add the strained
contents of a Pot of Tea. Stir well and
decorate with fruits in season. Serve
in 4 oz. Punch glasses.

CHAMPAGNE
PUNCH

CHAMPAGNE VELVET	See BLACK VELVET
CHAMPS ELYSEES COCKTAIL	1 oz. Cognac ½ oz. Yellow Chartreuse Juice of ¼ Lemon ½ Teaspoon Powdered Sugar 1 Dash Bitters Shake well with cracked Ice and strain into 3 oz. Cocktail glass.
CHARLES COCKTAIL	1¼ oz. Italian Vermouth 1¼ oz. Brandy 1 Dash Bitters Stir well with cracked Ice and strain into 3 oz. Cocktail glass.
CHELSEA SIDE CAR COCKTAIL	Juice of ¼ Lemon ¾ oz. Triple Sec ¾ oz. Dry Gin Shake well with cracked Ice and strain into 3 oz. Cocktail glass.
CHERRY BLOSSOM COCKTAIL	1 oz. Wild Cherry Flavored Brandy 1 oz. Brandy ¼ Teaspoon Curacao ¼ Teaspoon Lemon Juice ¼ Teaspoon Grenadine Shake well with cracked Ice and strain into 3 oz. Cocktail glass.
CHERRY FIZZ	Juice ½ Lemon 2 oz. Wild Cherry Flavored Brandy Shake well with cracked Ice and strain into 7 oz. Highball glass. Fill with Carbonated Water and decorate with a Cherry.

44

1 Egg
1 Teaspoon Powdered Sugar
1½ oz. Wild Cherry Flavored Brandy
2 Teaspoons Sweet Cream
  (if desired)
Shake well with cracked Ice and strain into 5 oz. Flip glass. Grate a little Nutmeg on top.

CHERRY FLIP

2 Cubes of Ice
1 oz. Wild Cherry Flavored Brandy
1 oz. Dry Gin
Serve in Old Fashioned Cocktail glass and stir. Twist of Lemon Peel and drop in glass.

CHERRY SLING

2 oz. Brandy
1 Dash Bitters
¼ Teaspoon Curacao
Shake well with cracked Ice and strain into 3 oz. Cocktail glass. Frost glass by rubbing slice of Lemon around rim and then dip in Powdered Sugar.

CHICAGO COCKTAIL

Juice ½ Lemon
1 Teaspoon Powdered Sugar
White of 1 Egg
1 oz. Port Wine
1 oz. Imported Rum
Shake well with cracked Ice and strain into 7 oz. Highball glass. Fill with Carbonated Water.

CHICAGO FIZZ

½ oz. Grenadine
1½ oz. Jamaica Rum
1 Dash Bitters
1 Teaspoon Maraschino
1 Teaspoon Curacao
Shake well with cracked Ice and strain into 3 oz. Cocktail glass.

CHINESE COCKTAIL

45

CHOCOLATE COCKTAIL	1½ oz. Port Wine ¼ oz. Yellow Chartreuse Yolk of 1 Egg 1 Teaspoon Powdered Sugar Shake well with cracked Ice and strain into 4 oz. Cocktail glass.
CHOCOLATE DAISY	Juice ½ Lemon ½ Teaspoon Powdered Sugar 1 Teaspoon Raspberry Syrup or Grenadine 1½ oz. Brandy 1½ oz. Port Wine Shake well with cracked Ice and strain into Stein or 8 oz. Metal Cup. Add Cube of Ice and decorate with Fruit.
CHOCOLATE FLIP	1 Egg 1 Teaspoon Powdered Sugar ¾ oz. Sloe Gin ¾ oz. Brandy 2 Teaspoons Sweet Cream (if desired) Shake well with cracked Ice and strain into 5 oz. Flip glass. Grate a little Nutmeg on top.
CHOCOLATE SOLDIER COCKTAIL	Juice ½ Lime ¾ oz. Dubonnet 1½ oz. Dry Gin Shake well with cracked Ice and strain into 3 oz. Cocktail glass.

CHRISTMAS YULE EGG NOG

Beat the yolks and whites of 1 Dozen Eggs separately and then pour together and add:
1 Pinch Baking Soda
6 oz. Imported Rum
2 lbs. Granulated Sugar and then beat into stiff batter. Then add:
1 qt. Milk
1 qt. Sweet Cream
2 qts. Rye or Bourbon Whiskey and stir. Set in refrigerator over night. Before serving, stir again, and serve in 4 oz. Punch glasses, and grate Nutmeg on top.

CHRYSANTHEMUM COCKTAIL

1 oz. Benedictine
1 oz. French Vermouth
1 Teaspoon Absinthe Substitute
Shake well with cracked Ice and strain into 3 oz. Cocktail glass.

CIDER CUP

Use Large Glass Pitcher
4 Teaspoons Powdered Sugar
6 oz. Carbonated Water
½ oz. Triple Sec
½ oz. Curacao
2 oz. Brandy
Fill pitcher with cubes of Ice. Add 1 Pint of Cider. Stir well and decorate with as many Fruits as available and also Rind of Cucumber inserted on each side of pitcher. Top with small bunch of Mint Sprigs. Serve in 5 oz. Claret glass.

CIDER EGG NOG

1 Egg
1 Teaspoon Powdered Sugar
¼ pt. Milk
Shake well with cracked Ice and strain into 12 oz. Tom Collins glass. Then fill glass with Sweet Cider. Grate Nutmeg on top.

CIRCUS RICKEY

1 Cube of Ice
Juice ½ Lime
½ Teaspoon Grenadine
1½ oz. Dry Gin
Fill 8 oz. Highball glass with Carbonated Water and stir. Leave Lime in glass.

CLARET COBBLER

1 Teaspoon Powdered Sugar
2 oz. Carbonated Water
3 oz. Claret
Fill 10 oz. Goblet with Shaved Ice and stir.
Decorate with fruits in season. Serve with straws.

CLARET CUP

Use Large Glass Pitcher
4 Teaspoons Powdered Sugar
6 oz. Carbonated Water
½ oz. Triple Sec
½ oz. Curacao
2 oz. Brandy
Fill pitcher with cubes of Ice. Add 1 Pint of Claret. Stir well and decorate with as many fruits as available and also Rind of Cucumber inserted on each side of pitcher. Top with small bunch of Mint Sprigs. Serve in 5 oz. Claret glass.

CLARET PUNCH

Juice of 1 Dozen Lemons
Add enough Powdered Sugar to sweeten
1 qt. Carbonated Water
Place large block of Ice in Punch Bowl and stir well. Then add:
½ pt. Curacao
1 pt. Brandy
3 qts. Claret
Some prefer to add the strained contents of a Pot of Tea. Stir well and decorate with fruits in season. Serve in 4 oz. Punch glasses.

¾ oz. Dry Gin
¾ oz. French Vermouth
½ oz. Apricot Flavored Brandy
½ oz. Triple Sec
Stir well with cracked Ice and strain
into 3 oz. Cocktail glass.

**CLARIDGE
COCKTAIL**

Juice of ¼ Lemon
¼ oz. Curacao
¼ oz. Maraschino
1 oz. Brandy
Shake well with cracked Ice and strain
into 3 oz. Cocktail glass. Frost rim of
glass by rubbing with Lemon and
dipping in Powdered Sugar.

CLASSIC COCKTAIL

1 oz. Italian Vermouth
½ oz. Sloe Gin
½ oz. Muscatel Wine
Shake well with cracked Ice and strain
into 3 oz. Cocktail glass.

CLOVE COCKTAIL

Juice ½ Lemon
2 Teaspoons Grenadine
White of 1 Egg
1½ oz. Dry Gin
Shake well with cracked Ice and strain
into 4 oz. Cocktail glass.

**CLOVER CLUB
COCKTAIL**

Juice 1 Lime
2 Teaspoons Grenadine
White of 1 Egg
1½ oz. Dry Gin
Shake well with cracked Ice and strain
into 4 oz. Cocktail glass. Serve with
Mint Leaf on top.

**CLOVER LEAF
COCKTAIL**

1½ oz. Dry Gin
¾ oz. Italian Vermouth
Stir well with cracked Ice and strain
into 3 oz. Cocktail glass. Add a Cherry
or Olive.

CLUB COCKTAIL

COBBLERS	See Index on page 5 for complete list of Cobbler recipes.
COFFEE COCKTAIL	1 Egg 1 Teaspoon Powdered Sugar 1 oz. Port Wine 1 oz. Brandy Shake well with cracked Ice and strain into 5 oz. Cocktail glass. Grate Nutmeg on top.
COFFEE FLIP	1 Egg 1 Teaspoon Powdered Sugar 1 oz. Brandy 1 oz. Port Wine 2 Teaspoons Sweet Cream (if desired) Shake well with cracked Ice and strain into 5 oz. Flip glass. Grate a little Nutmeg on top.
COGNAC HIGHBALL	1 Cube of Ice 2 oz. Cognac Fill 8 oz. Highball glass with Ginger Ale or Carbonated Water. Add twist of Lemon Peel, if desired, and stir gently.
COLD DECK COCKTAIL	½ oz. Creme de Menthe (White) ½ oz. Italian Vermouth 1 oz. Brandy Shake well with cracked Ice and strain into 3 oz. Cocktail glass.
COLLINS	See Index on page 13 for complete list of Collins recipes.
COLONIAL COCKTAIL	½ oz. Grapefruit Juice 1 Teaspoon Maraschino 1½ oz. Dry Gin Shake well with cracked Ice and strain into 3 oz. Cocktail glass. Serve with an Olive.

Juice ½ Lime or ¼ Lemon
1 Teaspoon Powdered Sugar
2 Dashes Orange Bitters
1½ oz. Rye or Bourbon Whiskey
Shake well with cracked Ice and strain
into 3 oz. Cocktail glass.

**COMMODORE
COCKTAIL**

See Index on page 13 for complete list
of Cooler recipes.

COOLERS

½ oz. French Vermouth
½ oz. Italian Vermouth
1 oz. Dry Gin
2 Sprigs Fresh Mint
Shake well with Cracked Ice and
strain into 3 oz. Cocktail glass.

**COOPERSTOWN
COCKTAIL**

½ Teaspoon Lemon Juice
1 Teaspoon Maraschino
White of 1 Egg
1½ oz. Dry Gin
Shake well with cracked Ice and strain
into 4 oz. Cocktail glass.

**CORNELL
COCKTAIL**

¾ oz. Dry Gin
¾ oz. Dubonnet
¾ oz. French Vermouth
Stir well with cracked Ice and strain
into 3 oz. Cocktail glass.

**CORONATION
COCKTAIL**

½ oz. Italian Vermouth
½ oz. Apple Brandy
1 oz. Brandy
Shake well with cracked Ice and strain
into 3 oz. Cocktail glass.

**CORPSE REVIVER
COCKTAIL**

51

COUNTRY CLUB COOLER

Into 12 oz. Tom Collins glass, put:
½ Teaspoon Grenadine
2 oz. Carbonated Water and stir
Fill glass with cracked Ice and add:
2 oz. French Vermouth
Fill with Carbonated Water or Ginger Ale
Insert spiral of Orange or Lemon Peel (or both) and dangle end over rim of glass.

COWBOY COCKTAIL

1½ oz. Rye or Bourbon Whiskey
½ oz. Sweet Cream
Shake well with cracked Ice and strain into 3 oz. Cocktail glass.

CREAM FIZZ

Juice ½ Lemon
1 Teaspoon Powdered Sugar
2 oz. Dry Gin
1 Teaspoon Fresh Cream
Shake well with cracked Ice and strain into 8 oz. Highball glass. Fill with Carbonated Water.

CREAM PUFF

2 oz. Imported Rum
1 oz. Sweet Cream
½ Teaspoon Powdered Sugar
Shake well with cracked Ice and strain into 8 oz. Highball glass. Fill with Carbonated Water and stir.

CREME DE GIN COCKTAIL

1½ oz. Dry Gin
½ oz. Creme de Menthe
White of 1 Egg
2 Teaspoons Lemon Juice
2 Teaspoons Orange Juice
Shake well with cracked Ice and strain into 4 oz. Cocktail glass.

1¼ oz. Rye or Bourbon Whiskey
1¼ oz. Madeira Wine
 1 Teaspoon Grenadine
Stir well with cracked Ice and strain
into 3 oz. Cocktail glass. Serve with 1
Green Cherry, 1 Red Cherry and 1
White Cherry.

**CREOLE LADY
COCKTAIL**

1½ oz. Dry Gin
 2 Teaspoons Lemon Juice
 1 Teaspoon Grenadine
Shake well with cracked Ice and strain
into 3 oz. Cocktail glass, leaving
enough room on top to float ¾ oz. Port
Wine.

• **CRIMSON
COCKTAIL**

 Juice of ¼ Lemon
 ¼ Teaspoon Grenadine
1½ oz. Rye or Bourbon Whiskey
Shake well with cracked Ice and strain
into 3 oz. Cocktail glass.

CROW COCKTAIL

 ½ oz. Creme de Yvette
 2 Dashes Orange Bitters
1½ oz. Dry Gin
Shake well with cracked Ice and strain
into 3 oz. Cocktail glass.

**CRYSTAL SLIPPER
COCKTAIL**

 Juice ½ Lime—Drop skin in glass
2 oz. Imported Rum
2 Cubes of Ice
 Fill glass with any Cola
Use 10 oz. glass and stir well.

CUBA LIBRE

 Juice of ½ Lime
 ½ Teaspoon Powdered Sugar
 2 oz. Imported Rum
Shake well with cracked Ice and strain
into 3 oz. Cocktail glass.

**CUBAN COCKTAIL
No. 1**

**CUBAN COCKTAIL
No. 2**

Juice of ½ Lime or ¼ Lemon
½ oz. Apricot Flavored Brandy
1½ oz. Brandy
1 Teaspoon Imported Rum
Shake well with cracked Ice and strain
into 3 oz. Cocktail glass.

**CUBAN SPECIAL
COCKTAIL**

½ oz. Pineapple Juice
Juice ½ Lime
1 oz. Imported Rum
½ Teaspoon Curacao
Shake well with cracked Ice and strain
into 3 oz. Cocktail glass. Decorate with
stick of Pineapple and a Cherry.

CUPID COCKTAIL

2 oz. Sherry Wine
1 Egg
1 Teaspoon Powdered Sugar
Shake well with cracked Ice and strain
into 5 oz. Cocktail glass. Grate a little
Nutmeg on top.

CUPS

See Index on page 13 for complete list
of Cup recipes.

**DAIQUIRI
COCKTAIL**

Juice 1 Lime
1 Teaspoon Powdered Sugar
1½ oz. Imported Rum
Shake well with cracked Ice and strain
into 3 oz. Cocktail glass.

DAISIES

See Index on page 13 for complete list
of Daisy recipes.

**DAMN—THE—
WEATHER
COCKTAIL**

1 Teaspoon Curacao
½ oz. Orange Juice
½ oz. Italian Vermouth
1 oz. Dry Gin
Shake well with cracked Ice and strain
into 3 oz. Cocktail glass.

1 oz. Rye or Bourbon Whiskey   **DANDY COCKTAIL**
1 oz. Dubonnet
1 Dash Bitters
1 Teaspoon Triple Sec
 Twist of Lemon Peel
 Twist of Orange Peel
Shake well with cracked Ice and strain
into 3 oz. Cocktail glass.

 1 Teaspoon Lemon Juice   **DARB COCKTAIL**
¾ oz. French Vermouth
¾ oz. Dry Gin
¾ oz. Apricot Flavored Brandy
Shake well with cracked Ice and strain
into 3 oz. Cocktail glass.

 Juice of ¼ Lemon   **DEAUVILLE**
½ oz. Brandy   **COCKTAIL**
½ oz. Apple Brandy
½ oz. Triple Sec
Shake well with cracked Ice and strain
into 3 oz. Cocktail glass.

1 oz. French Vermouth   **DEEP SEA**
¼ Teaspoon Absinthe Substitute **COCKTAIL**
1 Dash Orange bitters
1 oz. Dry Gin
Shake well with cracked ice and strain
into 3 oz. Cocktail glass.

1 oz. Dry Gin   **DEMPSEY**
1 oz. Apple Brandy   **COCKTAIL**
½ Teaspoon Absinthe Substitute
½ Teaspoon Grenadine
Shake well with cracked Ice and strain
into 3 oz. Cocktail glass.

DEPTH BOMB
COCKTAIL

¼ Teaspoon Lemon Juice
1 Teaspoon Grenadine
1 oz. Apple Brandy
1 oz. Brandy
Shake well with cracked Ice and strain into 3 oz. Cocktail glass.

DERBY FIZZ

Juice ½ Lemon
1 Teaspoon Powdered Sugar
1 Egg
2 oz. Scotch Whiskey
1 Teaspoon Curacao
Shake well with cracked Ice and strain into 8 oz. Highball glass. Fill with Carbonated Water.

DEVIL'S
COCKTAIL

½ Teaspoon Lemon Juice
1¼ oz. Port Wine
1¼ oz. French Vermouth
Stir well with cracked Ice and strain into 3 oz. Cocktail glass.

DIAMOND FIZZ

Juice ½ Lemon
1 Teaspoon Powdered Sugar
2 oz. Dry Gin
Shake well with cracked Ice and strain into 7 oz. Highball glass. Fill with Champagne.

DIANA COCKTAIL

Fill 3 oz. Cocktail glass with shaved Ice, then fill ¾ full with Creme de Menthe (White) and float California Brandy on top.

DICK,JR.
COCKTAIL

Juice of 1 Lime
½ oz. French Vermouth
¾ oz. Dry Gin
½ oz. Apricot Flavored Brandy
Shake well with cracked Ice and strain into 3 oz. Cocktail glass.

Juice of ¼ Lemon
½ Teaspoon Powdered Sugar
1½ oz. Rye or Bourbon Whiskey
2 or 3 Sprigs Fresh Mint
Shake very well with cracked Ice and
strain into 3 oz. Cocktail glass. Serve
with a Mint Leaf.

1½ oz. French Vermouth
½ oz. Italian Vermouth
2 Dashes Bitters
½ Teaspoon Maraschino
Shake well with cracked Ice and strain
into 3 oz. Cocktail glass. Serve with ½
Slice of Lemon and a Cherry.

Juice of ¼ Orange
½ oz. Absinthe Substitute
½ oz. French Vermouth
1 oz. Dry Gin
Shake well with cracked Ice and strain
into 4 oz. Cocktail glass.

Into a 12 oz. Tom Collins glass put
4 Sprigs of Mint
1 Teaspoon Powdered Sugar
2½ oz. Bourbon Whiskey
Fill with Shaved Ice and stir gently
until glass is frosted. Decorate with
Sprigs of Mint. Serve with straws.

½ Lump of Sugar
1 Dash Bitters
¼ Teaspoon Curacao
½ Teaspoon Creme de Menthe
2 oz. Rye or Bourbon Whiskey
Shake well with cracked Ice and strain
into 3 oz. Cocktail glass.

DOCTOR COCKTAIL

Juice ¼ Lemon
¾ oz. Dry Gin
¾ oz. Swedish Punch
Shake well with cracked Ice and strain into 3 oz. Cocktail glass.

DOG DAYS HIGHBALL

1 Cube of Ice
2 oz. Scotch Whiskey
Fill 8 oz. Highball glass with Ginger Ale or Carbonated Water. Add Twist of Lemon Peel, if desired, and stir gently.

DOUBLE STANDARD SOUR

Juice ½ Lemon or 1 Lime
½ Teaspoon Powdered Sugar
¾ oz. Rye or Bourbon Whiskey
¾ oz. Dry Gin
½ Teaspoon Raspberry Syrup or Grenadine
Shake well with cracked Ice and strain into 6 oz. Sour glass. Fill with Carbonated Water. Decorate with a half-slice of Lemon and a Cherry.

DREAM COCKTAIL

¾ oz. Curacao
1½ oz. Brandy
¼ Teaspoon Anisette
Shake well with cracked Ice and strain into 3 oz. Cocktail glass.

DRY MARTINI COCKTAIL

1½ oz. Dry Gin
¾ oz. French Vermouth
1 Dash Orange Bitters
Stir well with cracked Ice and strain into 3 oz. Cocktail glass. Serve with an Olive.

58

1 Dash Bitters
¾ oz. French Vermouth
½ Teaspoon Absinthe Substitute
1½ oz. Dry Gin
Shake well with cracked Ice and strain
into 3 oz. Cocktail glass. Add slice of
Orange.

**DU BARRY
COCKTAIL**

1½ oz. Dubonnet
¾ oz. Dry Gin
1 Dash Orange Bitters may be
added
Stir well with cracked Ice and strain
into 3 oz. Cocktail glass. Twist of
Lemon Peel on top and drop in glass.

**DUBONNET
COCKTAIL**

Juice ½ Orange
Juice ¼ Lemon
1 Teaspoon Wild Cherry Flavored
Brandy
2 oz. Dubonnet
Shake well with cracked Ice and strain
into 7 oz. Highball glass. Fill with
Carbonated Water.

DUBONNET FIZZ

1 Cube of Ice
2 oz. Dubonnet
Fill 8 oz. Highball glass with Ginger
Ale or Carbonated Water. Add twist
of Lemon Peel, if desired, and stir
gently.

**DUBONNET
HIGHBALL**

¾ oz. French Vermouth
¾ oz. Italian Vermouth
¾ oz. Absinthe Substitute
Stir well with cracked Ice and strain
into 3 oz. Cocktail glass.

**DUCHESS
COCKTAIL**

59

DUKE COCKTAIL

½ oz. Triple Sec
1 Teaspoon Orange Juice
2 Teaspoons Lemon Juice
½ Teaspoon Maraschino
1 Egg
Shake well with cracked Ice and strain into 8 oz. Stem glass and fill with Champagne.

DUNLOP COCKTAIL

¾ oz. Sherry Wine
1 Dash Bitters
1½ oz. Imported Rum
Stir well with cracked Ice and strain into 3 oz. Cocktail glass.

DUTCH MIKE

2 oz. Dry Gin
½ Teaspoon Amer Picon
Juice ½ Lime
Shake well with cracked Ice and strain into 12 oz. Tom Collins glass and fill with Carbonated Water.

EAST INDIA COCKTAIL No. 1

1½ oz. Brandy
½ Teaspoon Pineapple Juice
½ Teaspoon Curacao
1 Teaspoon Jamaica Rum
1 Dash Bitters
Shake well with cracked Ice and strain into 3 oz. Cocktail glass. Twist of Lemon Peel and add a Cherry.

EAST INDIA COCKTAIL No. 2

1¼ oz. French Vermouth
1¼ oz. Sherry Wine
1 Dash Orange Bitters
Stir well with cracked Ice and strain into 3 oz. Cocktail glass.

1 oz. Dry Gin
2 oz. Sloe Gin
½ Teaspoon Lemon Juice
Put enough Grenadine into 4 oz.
Cocktail glass to cover a ripe Olive.
Mix the above ingredients in Ice and
pour gently onto the Grenadine so that
they do not mix.

ECLIPSE COCKTAIL

See Index on page 13 for complete list
of Egg Nogg recipes.

EGG NOGGS

1 Egg
1 Teaspoon Powdered Sugar
Juice ½ Lemon
2 oz. Brandy
¼ Teaspoon Curacao
Shake well with cracked Ice and
strain into 8 oz. Highball glass.

EGG SOUR

White of 1 Egg
1½ oz. Rye or Bourbon Whiskey
¾ oz. Port Wine
Juice ¼ Lemon
1 Teaspoon Powdered Sugar
Add a strip of Pineapple
Shake well with cracked Ice and strain
into 4 oz. Cocktail glass.

ELK'S OWN COCKTAIL

Juice 1 Lime
1 Teaspoon Pineapple Juice
1 Teaspoon Grenadine
1½ oz. Imported Rum
Shake well with cracked Ice and strain
into 3 oz. Cocktail glass.

EL PRESIDENTE COCKTAIL No. 1

¾ oz. French Vermouth
1½ oz. Imported Rum
1 Dash Bitters
Shake well with cracked Ice and strain
into 3 oz. Cocktail glass.

EL PRESIDENTE COCKTAIL No. 2

EMERALD ISLE COCKTAIL	2 oz. Dry Gin 1 Teaspoon Creme de Menthe (Green) 3 Dashes Bitters Stir well with cracked Ice and strain into 3 oz. Cocktail glass.
ENGLISH HIGHBALL	1 Cube of Ice ¾ oz. Dry Gin ¾ oz. Brandy ¾ oz. Italian Vermouth Fill 8 oz. Highball glass with Ginger Ale or Carbonated Water. Add Twist of Lemon Peel, if desired, and stir gently.
ENGLISH ROSE COCKTAIL	1¼ oz. Dry Gin ¾ oz. Apricot Flavored Brandy ¾ oz. French Vermouth 1 Teaspoon Grenadine ¼ Teaspoon Lemon Juice Shake well with cracked Ice and strain into 4 oz. Cocktail glass. Frost rim of glass by rubbing with Lemon and dipping in Sugar. Serve with a Cherry.
ETHEL DUFFY COCKTAIL	¾ oz. Apricot Flavored Brandy ¾ oz. Creme de Menthe (White) ¾ oz. Curacao Shake well with cracked ice and strain into 3 oz. Cocktail glass.
EVERYBODY'S IRISH COCKTAIL	1 Teaspoon Creme de Menthe (Green) 1 Teaspoon Green Chartreuse 2 oz. Irish Whiskey Stir well with cracked Ice and strain into 3 oz. Cocktail glass. Serve with Green Olive.

Yolk of 1 Egg
½ Teaspoon Powdered Sugar
1 Teaspoon Absinthe Substitute
1 Teaspoon Curacao
1 Teaspoon Creme de Cacao
2 oz. Imported Rum
Shake well with cracked Ice and strain
into 4 oz. Cocktail glass.

**EYEOPENER
COCKTAIL**

¾ oz. Italian Vermouth
1½ oz. Imported Rum
½ Teaspoon Curacao
Stir well with cracked Ice and strain
into 3 oz. Cocktail glass.

**FAIR & WARMER
COCKTAIL**

White of 1 Egg
1 Teaspoon Grenadine
¾ oz. Apricot Flavored Brandy
1½ oz. Dry Gin
Shake well with cracked Ice and strain
into 4 oz. Cocktail glass.

**FAIRY BELLE
COCKTAIL**

Juice of 1 Lemon or ½ Lime
1½ oz. Dry Gin
1 Dash Bitters
½ Teaspoon Creme de Menthe
Shake well with cracked Ice and strain
into 3 oz. Cocktail glass. Serve with a
Cherry.

**FALLEN ANGEL
COCKTAIL**

2 oz. Brandy
1 Dash Bitters
¼ Teaspoon Curacao
¼ Teaspoon Powdered Sugar
Stir well with cracked Ice and strain
into 3 oz. Cocktail glass. Twist of
Lemon Peel and drop in glass.

**FANCY BRANDY
COCKTAIL**

**FANCY GIN
COCKTAIL**

2 oz. Dry Gin
1 Dash Bitters
¼ Teaspoon Curacao
¼ Teaspoon Powdered Sugar
Stir well with cracked Ice and strain
into 3 oz. Cocktail glass. Twist of
Lemon Peel and drop in glass.

**FANCY WHISKEY
COCKTAIL**

2 oz. Rye or Bourbon Whiskey
1 Dash Bitters
¼ Teaspoon Curacao
¼ Teaspoon Powdered Sugar
Stir well with cracked Ice and strain
into 3 oz. Cocktail glass. Twist of
Lemon Peel and drop in glass.

**FANTASIO
COCKTAIL**

1 Teaspoon Creme de Menthe
(White)
1 Teaspoon Maraschino
1 oz. Brandy
¾ oz. French Vermouth
Stir well with cracked Ice and strain
into 3 oz. Cocktail glass.

**FARMER'S
COCKTAIL**

1 oz. Dry Gin
½ oz. French Vermouth
½ oz. Italian Vermouth
2 Dashes Bitters
Shake well with cracked Ice and strain
into 3 oz. Cocktail glass.

**FASCINATOR
COCKTAIL**

¾ oz. French Vermouth
1½ oz. Dry Gin
½ Teaspoon Absinthe Substitute
1 Sprig Fresh Mint
Shake well with cracked Ice and strain
into 3 oz. Cocktail glass.

¾ oz. Apricot Flavored Brandy
¾ oz. French Vermouth
¾ oz. Dry Gin
¼ Teaspoon Lemon Juice
Shake well with cracked Ice and strain
into 3 oz. Cocktail glass.

FAVOURITE COCKTAIL

⅓ oz. Creme de Cacao
⅓ oz. Apricot Nectar
⅓ oz. Sweet Cream
Pour carefully, in order given, into
Pousse Cafe glass, so that each
ingredient floats on preceding one.

FIFTH AVENUE

1¼ oz. Dry Gin
1¼ oz. French Vermouth
Stir well with cracked Ice and strain
into 3 oz. Cocktail glass.

FIFTY-FIFTY COCKTAIL

Juice of ¼ Lemon
½ oz. Triple Sec
1¼ oz. Dry Gin
1 Dash Bitters
Shake well with cracked Ice and strain
into 3 oz. Cocktail glass. Serve with a
Cherry.

FINE AND DANDY COCKTAIL

Juice 2 Limes
½ Teaspoon Powdered Sugar
½ oz. Grenadine
2 oz. Imported Rum
Shake well with cracked Ice and strain
into Delmonico glass. Fill with
Carbonated Water, if desired. Decorate with a half-slice of Lemon and a
Cherry.

FIREMAN'S SOUR

FISH HOUSE PUNCH

Juice of 1 Dozen Lemons
Add enough Powdered Sugar to sweeten
1 qt. Carbonated Water
Place large block of Ice in Punch bowl and stir well.
Then add:
1½ qts. Brandy
1 pt. Peach Flavored Brandy
1 pt. Imported Rum
Some prefer to add the strained contents of a Pot of Tea. Stir well and decorate with fruits in season. Serve in 4 oz. Punch glasses.

FIXES

See Index on page 13 for complete list of Fix recipes.

FIZZES

See Index on page 13 for complete list of Fizz recipes.

FLAMINGO COCKTAIL

Juice of ½ Lime
½ oz. Apricot Nectar Liqueur
1¼ oz. Dry Gin
1 Teaspoon Grenadine
Shake well with cracked Ice and strain into 3 oz. Cocktail glass.

FLIPS

See Index on page 14 for complete list of Flip recipes.

FLORADORA COOLER

Into 12 oz. Tom Collins glass, put:
Juice 1 Lime
½ Teaspoon Powdered Sugar
½ oz. Raspberry Syrup or Grenadine
2 oz. Carbonated Water, and stir.
Fill glass with cracked Ice and add:
2 oz. Dry Gin.
Fill with Carbonated Water or Ginger Ale.

66

1¼ oz. Imported Rum
1¼ oz. Italian Vermouth
Stir well with cracked Ice and strain
into 3 oz. Cocktail glass after inserting
rind of Lime.

**FLUFFY RUFFLES
COCKTAIL**

1 oz. Italian Vermouth
1 oz. Scotch Whiskey
1 Dash Bitters
¼ Teaspoon Simple Syrup
Stir well with cracked Ice and strain
into 3 oz. Cocktail glass.

**FLYING
SCOTCHMAN
COCKTAIL**

1 Cube of Ice
Juice of ½ Lime
1½ oz. Dry Gin
Fill 8 oz. Highball glass with Ginger
Ale and stir. Leave lime in glass.

FOG HORN

¾ oz. French Vermouth
¾ oz. Dry Gin
¾ oz. Italian Vermouth
1 Teaspoon Absinthe Substitute
Shake well with cracked Ice and strain
into 3 oz. Cocktail glass. Serve with a
Cherry.

**FOURTH DEGREE
COCKTAIL**

½ oz. Creme de Cacao
2 oz. Rye or Bourbon Whiskey
4 Dashes Bitters
Stir well with cracked Ice and strain
into 3 oz. Cocktail glass.

**FOX RIVER
COCKTAIL**

1 oz. Dry Gin
¾ oz. French Vermouth
½ oz. Apricot Flavored Brandy
1 Teaspoon Triple Sec
Stir well with cracked Ice and strain
into 3 oz. Cocktail glass. Serve with a
Cherry.

**FRANKENJACK
COCKTAIL**

67

FRENCH "75"

Juice of 1 Lemon
2 Teaspoons Powdered Sugar
1 Cube of Ice
Stir well in 12 oz. Tom Collins glass.
Then add 2 oz. Dry Gin and fill with
Champagne. Decorate with slice of
Lemon, Orange and a Cherry. Serve
with straws.

FRISCO SOUR

Juice ¼ Lemon
Juice ½ Lime
½ oz. Raspberry Syrup or Grenadine
2 oz. Rye or Bourbon Whiskey
Shake well with cracked Ice and strain
into 6 oz. Sour glass. Fill with
Carbonated Water.

**FROSTED DAIQUIRI
COCKTAIL**

See West Indies Frosted Cocktail on
Page 149.

**FROTH BLOWER
COCKTAIL**

White of 1 Egg
1 Teaspoon Grenadine
2 oz. Dry Gin
Shake well with cracked Ice and strain
into 4 oz. Cocktail glass.

**FROUPE
COCKTAIL**

1¼ oz. Italian Vermouth
1¼ oz. Brandy
1 Teaspoon Benedictine
Stir well with cracked Ice and
strain into 3 oz. Cocktail glass.

**GASPER
COCKTAIL**

1 oz. Dry Gin
1 oz. Apricot Flavored Brandy
If desired add a very little Powdered
Sugar. Shake well with cracked Ice
and strain into 3 oz. Cocktail glass.

1 oz. Italian Vermouth
1 oz. Brandy
1 Teaspoon Powdered Sugar
1 Teaspoon Lemon Juice
Shake well with cracked Ice and strain
into 3 oz. Cocktail glass.

GAZETTE COCKTAIL

1 Egg
1 Teaspoon Powdered Sugar
Shake well with cracked Ice and strain
into 12 oz. Tom Collins glass. Fill glass
with Claret or Sweet Cider. Grate
Nutmeg on top.

GENERAL HARRISON'S EGG NOG

1½ oz. Dry Gin
½ oz. French Vermouth
Shake well with cracked Ice and strain
into 3 oz. Cocktail Glass. Twist of
Lemon Peel and serve with 3 Pearl
Onions.

GIBSON COCKTAIL

Juice of ¼ Lemon
½ oz. French Vermouth
¾ oz. Wild Cherry Flavored Brandy
¾ oz. Dry Gin
1 Dash Orange Bitters
Stir well with cracked Ice and strain
into 3 oz. Cocktail glass.

GILROY COCKTAIL

Juice 1 Lime
1 Teaspoon Powdered Sugar
1½ oz. Dry Gin
Shake well with cracked Ice and strain
into 4 oz. Cocktail glass and fill balance
with Carbonated Water.

GIMLET COCKTAIL

Put ½ Teaspoon Bitters into 3 oz.
Cocktail glass and revolve glass until
it is entirely coated with the Bitters.
Then fill with Dry Gin. No Ice is used
in this drink.

GIN AND BITTERS

69

GIN AND IT [**English**]	2 oz. Dry Gin 1 oz. Italian Vermouth Stir. No Ice is used in this drink. Serve in 3 oz. Cocktail glass.
GIN and TONIC	2 oz. Dry Gin Cube of Ice Fill glass with Quinine Tonic and stir. Use 12 oz. Tom Collins glass.
GIN BUCK	1 Cube of Ice Juice of ½ Lemon 1½ oz. Dry Gin Fill 8 oz. Highball glass with Ginger Ale and stir.
GIN COBBLER	1 Teaspoon Powdered Sugar 2 oz. Carbonated Water Fill 10 oz. Goblet with Shaved Ice Add 2 oz. Dry Gin Stir well and decorate with fruits in season. Serve with straws.
GIN COCKTAIL	2 oz. Dry Gin 2 Dashes Bitters Stir well with cracked Ice and strain into 3 oz. Cocktail glass. Serve with a Twist of Lemon Peel and drop in glass.
GIN COOLER	Into 12 oz. Tom Collins glass, put: ½ Teaspoon Powdered Sugar 2 oz. Carbonated Water, and stir Fill glass with cracked Ice and add: 2 oz. Dry Gin Fill with Carbonated Water or Ginger Ale Insert spiral of Orange or Lemon Peel (or both) and dangle end over rim of glass.

GIN DAISY

Juice of ½ Lemon
½ Teaspoon Powdered Sugar
1 Teaspoon Raspberry Syrup or Grenadine
2 oz. Dry Gin
Shake well with cracked Ice and strain into Stein or 8 oz. metal cup. Add Cube of Ice and decorate with fruit.

GIN FIX

Juice ½ Lemon
1 Teaspoon Powdered Sugar
1 Teaspoon Water and stir
Fill glass with Shaved Ice
2½ oz. Dry Gin
Use 12 oz. Tom Collins glass. Stir well. Add slice of Lemon. Serve with straws.

GIN FIZZ

Juice ½ Lemon
1 Teaspoon Powdered Sugar
2 oz. Dry Gin
Shake well with cracked Ice and strain into 7 oz. Highball glass. Fill with Carbonated Water.

GIN HIGHBALL

1 Cube of Ice
2 oz. Dry Gin
Fill 8 oz. Highball glass with Ginger Ale or Carbonated Water. Add twist of Lemon Peel, if desired, and stir gently.

GIN MILK PUNCH

1 Teaspoon Powdered Sugar
2 oz. Dry Gin
½ pt. Milk
Shake well with cracked Ice, strain into 12 oz. Tom Collins glass and grate Nutmeg on top.

GIN RICKEY

1 Cube of Ice
Juice of ½ Lime
1½ oz. Dry Gin
Fill 8 oz. Highball glass with Carbonated Water and stir. Leave Lime in glass.

GIN SANGAREE	1½ oz. Dry Gin 1 Teaspoon Powdered Sugar Shake well with cracked Ice and strain into 3 oz. Cocktail glass, leaving enough room in which to float a tablespoon of Port Wine.
GIN SLING	Dissolve 1 Teaspoon Powdered Sugar in Teaspoon of Water. 2 oz. Dry Gin 2 Cubes of Ice Serve in Old Fashioned Cocktail glass and stir. Twist of Orange Peel and drop in glass.
GIN SMASH	Muddle 1 Lump of Sugar with 1 oz. Carbonated Water and 4 Sprigs of Green Mint Add 2 oz. Dry Gin, then a Cube of Ice. Stir and decorate with a slice of Orange and a Cherry. Twist Lemon Peel on top. use Old Fashioned Cocktail glass.
GIN SOUR	Juice ½ Lemon ½ Teaspoon Powdered Sugar 2 oz. Dry Gin Shake well with cracked Ice and strain into 6 oz. Sour glass. Fill with Carbonated Water. Decorate with a half-slice of Lemon and a Cherry.
GIN SQUIRT	1½ oz. Dry Gin 1 Tablespoon Powdered Sugar 1 Teaspoon Raspberry Syrup or Grenadine Stir well with cracked Ice and strain into 8 oz. Highball glass and fill with Carbonated Water. Decorate with cubes of Pineapple and Strawberries.

Into 12 oz. Tom Collins glass, put:
Juice 1 Lime
1 Teaspoon Powdered Sugar
2 oz. Carbonated Water
Fill glass with shaved Ice and stir
thoroughly with swizzle stick. Then
add:
2 Dashes Bitters
2 oz. Dry Gin
Fill with Carbonated Water and serve
with swizzle stick in glass, allowing
individual to do final stirring.

GIN SWIZZLE

Use Old Fashioned Cocktail glass.
½ Teaspoon Powdered Sugar
2 Teaspoons Water
2 oz. Dry Gin
1 Lump of Ice
Stir well and Twist Lemon Peel on top.

GIN TODDY

Put Lump of Sugar into Hot Whiskey
glass and fill with two-thirds Boiling
Water. Add 2 oz. Dry Gin. Stir and
decorate with slice of Lemon. Grate
Nutmeg on top.

**GIN TODDY
[Hot]**

Juice of ½ Lemon
1 Teaspoon Powdered Sugar
2 oz. Dry Gin
Yolk of 1 Egg
Shake well with cracked Ice and strain
into 8 oz. Highball glass. Fill with
Carbonated Water.

GOLDEN FIZZ

1½ oz. Dry Gin
1 Scoop Orange Sherbet
Shake well and strain into 4 oz.
Cocktail glass.

**GOLDEN GATE
COCKTAIL**

73

GOLDEN MARTINI COCKTAIL

1½ oz. Orange Flavored Gin
¾ oz. French Vermouth
Stir well with cracked Ice and strain into 3 oz. Cocktail glass. Serve with an Olive.

GOLDEN SLIPPER COCKTAIL

¾ oz. Yellow Chartreuse
2 oz. Apricot Nectar Liqueur
Shake well with cracked Ice and strain into 4 oz. Cocktail glass. Float Yolk of Egg on top.

GOLF COCKTAIL

1½ oz. Dry Gin
¾ oz. French Vermouth
2 Dashes Bitters
Stir well with cracked Ice and strain into 3 oz. Cocktail glass.

GRAND ROYAL FIZZ

Juice ¼ Orange
Juice ½ Lemon
1 Teaspoon Powdered Sugar
2 oz. Dry Gin
½ Teaspoon Maraschino
2 Teaspoons Sweet Cream
Shake well with cracked Ice and strain into 8 oz. Highball glass. Fill with Carbonated Water.

GRAPEFRUIT COCKTAIL

1 oz. Grapefruit Juice
1 oz. Dry Gin
1 Teaspoon Maraschino
Shake well with cracked Ice and strain into 3 oz. Cocktail glass. Serve with a Cherry.

GRAPE VINE COCKTAIL

Juice ¼ Lemon
½ oz. Grape Juice
1¼ oz. Dry Gin
¼ Teaspoon Grenadine
Stir well with cracked Ice and strain into 3 oz. Cocktail glass.

Juice of ¼ Lemon
½ oz. Kummel
½ oz. Creme de Menthe (Green)
1½ oz. Dry Gin
4 Dashes Orange bitters
Shake well with cracked Ice and strain
into 4 oz. Cocktail glass.

**GREEN DRAGON
COCKTAIL**

1 Teaspoon Powdered Sugar
White 1 Egg
Juice ½ Lemon
2 oz. Dry Gin
1 Teaspoon Creme de Menthe (Green)
Shake well with cracked Ice and strain
into 8 oz. Highball glass. Fill with
Carbonated Water.

GREEN FIZZ

¾ oz. Brandy
1½ oz. French Vermouth
½ Teaspoon Curacao
Shake well with cracked Ice and strain
into 3 oz. Cocktail glass.

**GREEN ROOM
COCKTAIL**

Made same as Gin Swizzle and add 1
Tablespoon Green Creme de Menthe.
If desired, Rum, Brandy or Whiskey
may be substituted for the Gin.

GREEN SWIZZLE

1 Cube of Ice
Juice ½ Lime
1½ oz. Grenadine
Fill 8 oz. Highball glass with
Carbonated Water and stir. Leave
Lime in glass.

**GRENADINE
RICKEY**

1¼ oz. Italian Vermouth
1¼ oz. Irish Whiskey
Stir well with cracked Ice and strain
into 3 oz. Cocktail glass.

GRIT COCKTAIL

GUARD'S COCKTAIL	¾ oz. Italian Vermouth
	1½ oz. Dry Gin
	½ Teaspoon Curacao
	Stir well with cracked Ice and strain into 3 oz. Cocktail glass. Serve with a Cherry.

GUARD'S COCKTAIL

¾ oz. Italian Vermouth
1½ oz. Dry Gin
½ Teaspoon Curacao
Stir well with cracked Ice and strain into 3 oz. Cocktail glass. Serve with a Cherry.

GYPSY COCKTAIL

1¼ oz. Italian Vermouth
1¼ oz. Dry Gin
Stir well with cracked Ice and strain into 3 oz. Cocktail glass. Serve with a Cherry.

HAKAM COCKTAIL

1¼ oz. Dry Gin
1¼ oz. Italian Vermouth
1 Dash Orange bitters
½ Teaspoon Curacao
Stir well with cracked Ice and strain into 3 oz. Cocktail glass. Serve with a Cherry.

HARLEM COCKTAIL

¾ oz. Pineapple Juice
1½ oz. Dry Gin
½ Teaspoon Maraschino
2 Cubes of Pineapple
Shake well with cracked Ice and strain into 3 oz. Cocktail glass.

HARRY LAUDER COCKTAIL

1¼ oz. Scotch Whiskey
1¼ oz. Italian Vermouth
½ Teaspoon Simple Syrup
Stir well with cracked Ice and strain into 3 oz. Cocktail glass.

HARVARD COCKTAIL

1½ oz. Brandy
¾ oz. Italian Vermouth
1 Dash Bitters
1 Teaspoon Grenadine
2 Teaspoons Lemon Juice
Stir well with cracked Ice and strain into 3 oz. Cocktail glass.

76

Into 12 oz. Tom Collins glass, put:
½ Teaspoon Powdered Sugar
2 oz. Carbonated Water, and stir.
Fill glass with cracked Ice and add:
2 oz. Applejack
Fill with Carbonated Water or
Ginger Ale
Insert spiral of Orange or Lemon Peel
(or both) and dangle end over rim of
glass.

HARVARD COOLER

¾ oz. French Vermouth
1½ oz. Dry Gin
¼ Teaspoon Absinthe Substitute
1 Teaspoon Grenadine
Stir well with cracked Ice and strain
into 3 oz. Cocktail glass.

HASTY COCKTAIL

1¼ oz. Pineapple Juice
¾ oz. Imported Rum
½ Teaspoon Lemon Juice
Shake well with cracked Ice and strain
into 3 oz. Cocktail glass.

HAVANA COCKTAIL

¾ oz. Swedish Punch
1½ oz. Dry Gin
½ Teaspoon Grenadine
Juice of ½ Lime
Shake well with cracked Ice and strain
into 4 oz. Cocktail glass. Serve with
Pineapple on edge with Cherry on
Pineapple.

HAVE A HEART COCKTAIL

2 oz. Dry Gin
½ oz. Pineapple Juice
½ oz. Curacao
Shake well with cracked Ice and strain
into 4 oz. Cocktail glass.

HAWAIIAN COCKTAIL

Take two Tom Collins glasses. Put a
teaspoonful of Bromo Seltzer into one
and fill the other half full of water.
Pour from one glass to the other until
thoroughly mixed and drink at once.

HEADACHE RELIEVER

HI-DE-HO SPECIAL

2 oz. Orange Flavored Gin
Juice of ½ Lemon
1 Teaspoon Powdered Sugar
Add cracked Ice, stir and strain into 8 oz. Highball glass. Then fill with Seltzer Water. Decorate with slice of Lemon.

HIGHBALLS

See Index on page 14 for complete list of Highball recipes.

HIGHLAND COOLER

Into 12 oz. Tom Collins glass, put:
½ Teaspoon Powdered Sugar
2 oz. Carbonated Water, and stir.
Fill glass with cracked Ice and add:
2 oz. Scotch Whiskey.
Fill with Carbonated Water or Ginger Ale
Insert spiral of Orange or Lemon Peel (or both) and dangle end over rim of glass.

HIGHLAND FLING COCKTAIL

¾ oz. Italian Vermouth
1½ oz. Scotch Whiskey
2 Dashes Orange Bitters
Shake well with cracked Ice and strain into 3 oz. Cocktail glass. Serve with an Olive.

HOFFMAN HOUSE COCKTAIL

¾ oz. French Vermouth
1½ oz. Dry Gin
2 Dashes Orange Bitters
Stir well with cracked Ice and strain into 3 oz. Cocktail glass. Serve with an Olive.

HOLE-IN-ONE COCKTAIL

1½ oz. Scotch Whiskey
¾ oz. French Vermouth
¼ Teaspoon Lemon Juice
1 Dash Orange bitters
Shake well with cracked Ice and strain into 3 oz. Cocktail glass.

1 Slice of Orange
1½ oz. Dry Gin
¾ oz. Italian Vermouth
Shake well with cracked Ice and strain
into 3 oz. Cocktail glass.

HOMESTEAD COCKTAIL

¾ oz. Benedictine
¾ oz. Apple Brandy
Juice of ½ Lemon
1 Teaspoon Curacao
Shake well with cracked Ice and strain
into 3 oz. Cocktail glass.

HONEYMOON COCKTAIL

1 Dash Bitters
¼ Teaspoon Orange Juice
¼ Teaspoon Pineapple Juice
¼ Teaspoon Lemon Juice
½ Teaspoon Powdered Sugar
1½ oz. Dry Gin
Shake well with cracked Ice and strain
into 3 oz. Cocktail glass.

HONOLULU COCKTAIL No. 1

¾ oz. Dry Gin
¾ oz. Maraschino
¾ oz. Benedictine
Stir well with cracked Ice and strain
into 3 oz. Cocktail glass.

HONOLULU COCKTAIL No. 2

¾ oz. Italian Vermouth
1½ oz. Scotch Whiskey
1 Teaspoon Benedictine
Stir well with cracked Ice and strain
into 3 oz. Cocktail glass. Twist of
Lemon Peel and drop in glass.

HOOT MON COCKTAIL

Juice ½ Lime
¾ oz. Apricot Flavored Brandy
¾ oz. Imported Rum
Stir well with cracked ice and strain
into 3 oz. Cocktail glass.

HOP TOAD COCKTAIL

79

HORSES NECK
[With a Kick]

Peel rind of whole Lemon in spiral fashion and put in 12 oz. Tom Collins glass with one end hanging over the rim. Fill glass with ice cubes. Add 2 oz. Rye or Bourbon Whiskey. Then fill with Ginger Ale and stir well.

HOT BRANDY
FLIP

1 Egg
1 Teaspoon Powdered Sugar
1½ oz. Brandy
Beat Egg, Sugar and Brandy and pour into hot Tom & Jerry Mug and fill with hot Milk. Grate Nutmeg on top.

HOT BRICK
TODDY

Into Hot Whiskey glass, put:
1 Teaspoon Butter
1 Teaspoon Powdered Sugar
3 Pinches Cinnamon
1 oz. Hot Water, and dissolve thoroughly. Then add:
1½ oz. Rye or Bourbon Whiskey
Fill with boiling Water and stir.

HOT BUTTERED
RUM

Put Lump of Sugar into Hot Whiskey glass and fill with two-thirds Boiling Water. Add square of Butter and 2 oz. Imported Rum. Stir and grate Nutmeg on top.

HOT SPRINGS
COCKTAIL

1½ oz. Dry White Wine
½ oz. Pineapple Juice
½ Teaspoon Maraschino
1 Dash Orange Bitters
Shake well with cracked Ice and strain into 3 oz. Cocktail glass.

HOT TODDIES

See Index on page 15 for complete list of Toddy recipes.

¾ oz. Italian Vermouth
¾ oz. French Vermouth
¾ oz. Dry Gin
Crush 1 Slice of Pineapple
Shake well with cracked Ice and strain
into 3 oz. Cocktail glass.

HOTEL PLAZA COCKTAIL

¼ oz. French Vermouth
¼ oz. Italian Vermouth
1½ oz. Dry Gin
Shake well with cracked Ice and strain
into 3 oz. Cocktail glass. Twist of
Orange Peel and drop in glass.

H. P. W. COCKTAIL

¾ oz. Orange Juice
1½ oz. Dry Gin
¼ Teaspoon Powdered Sugar
Shake well with cracked Ice and strain
into 3 oz. Cocktail glass.

HULA-HULA COCKTAIL

½ oz. Rye or Bourbon Whiskey
½ oz. Dry Gin
½ oz. Creme de Menthe
Juice of ½ Lemon
Shake well with cracked Ice and strain
into 3 oz. Cocktail glass.

HURRICANE COCKTAIL

1 Egg
1 oz. Maraschino
1 oz. Curacao
1 Small Scoop Vanilla Ice Cream
Shake well with cracked Ice and strain
into 5 oz. Flip glass Grate a little
Nutmeg on top.

ICE CREAM FLIP

1 oz. French Vermouth
1 oz. Dry Gin
¼ Teaspoon Maraschino
½ Teaspoon Grapefruit or Lemon
Juice.
Shake well with cracked Ice and strain
into 3 oz. Cocktail glass. Serve with a
Cherry.

IDEAL COCKTAIL

81

IMPERIAL COCKTAIL

1¼ oz. French Vermouth
1¼ oz. Dry Gin
¼ Teaspoon Maraschino
1 Dash Bitters
Stir well with cracked Ice and strain into 3 oz. Cocktail glass. Serve with a Cherry.

IMPERIAL FIZZ

Juice ½ Lemon
½ oz. Imported Rum
1½ oz. Rye or Bourbon Whiskey
1 Teaspoon Powdered Sugar
Shake well with cracked Ice and strain into 7 oz. Highball glass. Fill with Carbonated Water.

INCOME TAX COCKTAIL

¼ oz. French Vermouth
¼ oz. Italian Vermouth
1 oz. Dry Gin
1 Dash Bitters
Juice of ¼ Orange
Shake well with cracked Ice and strain into 3 oz. Cocktail glass.

IRISH RICKEY

1 Cube of Ice
Juice of ½ Lime
1½ oz. Irish Whiskey
Fill 8 oz. Highball glass with Carbonated Water and stir. Leave Lime in glass.

IRISH SHILLELAH

Juice ½ Lemon
1 Teaspoon Powdered Sugar
1½ oz. Irish Whiskey
½ oz. Sloe Gin
½ oz. Imported Rum
2 Slices of Peach
Shake well with cracked Ice and strain into 5 oz. Punch glass. Decorate with Fresh Raspberries, Strawberries and a Cherry.

½ Teaspoon Curacao
½ Teaspoon Absinthe Substitute
¼ Teaspoon Maraschino
1 Dash Bitters
2 oz. Irish Whiskey
Stir well with cracked Ice and strain
into 3 oz. Cocktail glass. Serve with an
Olive.

**IRISH WHISKEY
COCKTAIL**

1 Cube of Ice
2 oz. Irish Whiskey
Fill 8 oz. Highball glass with Ginger
Ale or Carbonated Water. Add twist
of Lemon Peel, if desired, and stir
gently.

**IRISH WHISKEY
HIGHBALL**

1 oz. Applejack
1 oz. Pineapple Juice
  Dash Bitters
Shake well with cracked Ice and strain
into 3 oz. Cocktail glass.

**JACK-IN-THE-BOX
COCKTAIL**

¾ oz. Dry Gin
¾ oz. French Vermouth
¼ oz. Apricot Nectar Liqueur
¼ oz. Triple Sec
Shake well with cracked Ice and strain
into 3 oz. Cocktail glass.

**JACK RABBIT
COCKTAIL**

1½ oz. Applejack
  Juice ½ Lime
1 Teaspoon Grenadine
Shake well with cracked Ice and strain
into 3 oz. Cocktail glass.

**JACK ROSE
COCKTAIL**

1 oz. Dry Gin
½ oz. Claret
½ oz. Orange Juice
1 Teaspoon Jamaica Rum
Shake well with cracked Ice and strain
into 3 oz. Cocktail glass.

**JAMAICA GLOW
COCKTAIL**

83

JAMAICA GRANITO

Small scoop of either Lemon or Orange Sherbert
1½ oz. Brandy
1 oz. Curacao
Use 12 oz. Tom Collins glass and fill balance with Carbonated Water and stir well. Grate Nutmeg on top.

JAPANESE FIZZ

Juice ½ Lemon
1 Teaspoon Powdered Sugar
1½ oz. Rye or Bourbon Whiskey
½ oz. Port Wine
White 1 Egg
Shake well with cracked Ice and strain into 8 oz. Highball glass. Fill with Carbonated Water. Serve with Slice of Pineapple.

JERSEY LIGHTNING COCKTAIL

1½ oz. Applejack
½ oz. Italian Vermouth
Juice 1 Lime
Shake well with cracked Ice and strain into 3 oz. Cocktail glass.

JEWEL COCKTAIL

¾ oz. Green Chartreuse
¾ oz. Italian Vermouth
¾ oz. Dry Gin
1 Dash Orange Bitters
Stir well with cracked Ice and strain into 3 oz. Cocktail glass. Serve with a Cherry.

JEYPLAK COCKTAIL

1½ oz. Dry Gin
¾ oz. Italian Vermouth
¼ Teaspoon Absinthe Substitute
Stir well with cracked Ice and strain into 3 oz. Cocktail glass. Serve with a Cherry.

1 Dash Bitters
¼ Teaspoon Creme de Cacao
Juice of ¼ Lemon
1½ oz. Dry Gin
Shake well with cracked Ice and strain
into 3 oz. Cocktail glass.

**JOCKEY CLUB
COCKTAIL**

Juice ½ Lemon
1 Teaspoon Powdered Sugar
2 oz. Holland Gin
Pour into 12 oz. Tom Collins glass. Add
several Cubes of Ice, fill with
Carbonated Water and stir well.
Decorate with slice of Orange, Lemon
and a Cherry. Serve with straws.

JOHN COLLINS

¾ oz. Curacao
1½ oz. Sloe Gin
1 Teaspoon Anisette
Stir well with cracked Ice and strain
into 3 oz. Cocktail glass.

**JOHNNIE
COCKTAIL**

¼ oz. French Vermouth
¼ oz. Italian Vermouth
1½ oz. Dry Gin
½ Teaspoon Lemon Juice
½ Teaspoon Curacao
1 Dash Bitters
Shake well with cracked Ice and strain
into 3 oz. Cocktail glass.

**JOURNALIST
COCKTAIL**

¾ oz. Dry Gin
¾ oz. Imported Rum
Juice of ¼ Lemon
½ Teaspoon Powdered Sugar
¼ Teaspoon Grenadine
Shake well with cracked Ice and strain
into 3 oz. Cocktail glass.

**JUDGE JR.
COCKTAIL**

JUDGETTE COCKTAIL	¾ oz. Peach Flavored Brandy
	¾ oz. Dry Gin
	¾ oz. French Vermouth
	Juice of ¼ Lime

JUDGETTE COCKTAIL

¾ oz. Peach Flavored Brandy
¾ oz. Dry Gin
¾ oz. French Vermouth
.   Juice of ¼ Lime
Shake well with cracked Ice and strain into 3 oz. Cocktail glass. Serve with a Cherry.

JULEPS

See Index on page 14 for complete list of Julep recipes.

JUPITER COCKTAIL

¾ oz. French Vermouth
1¼ oz. Dry Gin
1 Teaspoon Orange Juice
1 Teaspoon Creme de Cacao
Shake well with cracked Ice and strain into 3 oz. Cocktail glass.

K. C. B. COCKTAIL

½ oz. Kummel
1½ oz. Dry Gin
¼ Teaspoon Apricot Flavored Brandy
¼ Teaspoon Lemon Juice
Shake well with cracked Ice and strain into 3 oz. Cocktail glass. Add Twist of Lemon Peel and drop in glass.

KENTUCKY COCKTAIL

1¼ oz. Pineapple Juice
¾ oz. Bourbon Whiskey
Shake well with cracked Ice and strain into 3 oz. Cocktail glass.

KENTUCKY COLONEL COCKTAIL

½ oz. Benedictine
1½ oz. Bourbon Whiskey
Twist of Lemon Peel
Stir well with cracked Ice and strain into a 3 oz. Cocktail glass.

1 Slice of Orange
1 Slice of Pineapple
½ Teaspoon Powdered Sugar
  Muddle well in Old Fashioned
  Cocktail glass and add:
2 oz. Rye or Bourbon Whiskey
1 Cube of Ice
Stir well.

KING COLE COCKTAIL

¾ oz. Dry Gin
¾ oz. Wild Cherry Flavored Brandy
¾ oz. French Vermouth
Stir well with cracked Ice and strain
into 3 oz. Cocktail glass.

KISS-IN-THE-DARK COCKTAIL

Into 12 oz. Tom Collins glass, put:
½ Teaspoon Powdered Sugar
2 oz. Carbonated Water, and stir.
  Fill glass with cracked Ice and add:
2 oz. Rye or Bourbon Whiskey.
  Fill with Carbonated Water or
  Ginger Ale
Insert Spiral of Orange or Lemon Peel
(or both) and dangle end over rim of
glass.

KLONDIKE COOLER

¾ oz. French Vermouth
1½ oz. Dry Gin
¼ Teaspoon Italian Vermouth
Stir well with cracked Ice and strain
into 3 oz. Cocktail glass. Add Twist of
Lemon Peel and drop in glass.

KNICKERBOCKER COCKTAIL

1 Teaspoon Raspberry Syrup
1 Teaspoon Lemon Juice
1 Teaspoon Orange Juice
2 oz. Imported Rum
½ Teaspoon Curacao
Shake well with cracked Ice and strain
into 4 oz. Cocktail glass. Decorate with
small slice of Pineapple.

KNICKERBOCKER SPECIAL COCKTAIL

87

KNOCK-OUT COCKTAIL

½ oz. Absinthe Substitute
¾ oz. Dry Gin
¾ oz. French Vermouth
1 Teaspoon Creme de Menthe (White)
Shake well with cracked Ice and strain into 3 oz. Cocktail glass. Serve with a Cherry.

KUP'S INDISPENSABLE COCKTAIL

½ oz. Italian Vermouth
½ oz. French Vermouth
1¼ oz. Dry Gin
1 Dash Bitters
Stir well with cracked Ice and strain into 3 oz. Cocktail glass.

LADIES' COCKTAIL

1¾ oz. Rye or Bourbon Whiskey
½ Teaspoon Absinthe Substitute
½ Teaspoon Anisette
2 Dashes Bitters
Shake well with cracked Ice and strain into 3 oz. Cocktail glass. Serve with a piece of Pineapple on top.

LADY LOVE FIZZ

1 Teaspoon Powdered Sugar
Juice of ½ Lemon
White of 1 Egg
2 oz. Dry Gin
2 Teaspoons Sweet Cream
Shake well with cracked Ice and strain into 8 oz. Highball glass. Fill with Carbonated Water.

LASKY COCKTAIL

¾ oz. Grape Juice
¾ oz. Swedish Punch
¾ oz. Dry Gin
Shake well with cracked Ice and strain into 3 oz. Cocktail glass.

3/4 oz. French Vermouth
1 1/2 oz. Rye or Bourbon Whiskey
1/4 Teaspoon Absinthe Substitute
1/4 Teaspoon Maraschino
1 Dash Bitters
Stir well with cracked Ice and strain
into 3 oz. Cocktail glass.

**LAWHILL
COCKTAIL**

Juice 1/2 Lemon
2 oz. Dry Gin
1 Cube of Ice
Fill 8 oz. Highball glass with Ginger
Ale and stir gently.

**LEAP FROG
HIGHBALL**

1 1/4 oz. Dry Gin
1/2 oz. Orange Flavored Gin
1/2 oz. Italian Vermouth
Shake well with cracked Ice and strain
into 3 oz. Cocktail glass.

**LEAP YEAR
COCKTAIL**

1/2 oz. Apricot Flavored Brandy
1/2 oz. French Vermouth
1 oz. Dry Gin
1/4 Teaspoon Lemon Juice
1/4 Teaspoon Grenadine
Shake well with cracked Ice and strain
into 3 oz. Cocktail glass.

**LEAVE IT TO ME
COCKTAIL No. 1**

1 Teaspoon Raspberry Syrup
1 Teaspoon Lemon Juice
1/4 Teaspoon Maraschino
1 1/2 oz. Dry Gin
Stir well with cracked Ice and strain
into 3 oz. Cocktail glass.

**LEAVE IT TO ME
COCKTAIL No. 2**

89

LEMON SQUASH

1 Lemon peeled and quartered
2 Teaspoons Powdered Sugar
Muddle well in 12 oz. Tom Collins glass until juice is well extracted. Then fill glass with cracked Ice and fill with Carbonated Water and stir well. Decorate with Fruits.

LEMONADE
[Carbonated]

Juice of 1 Lemon
2 Teaspoons Powdered Sugar
Fill 12 oz. Tom Collins glass with shaved Ice. Add enough Carbonated Water to fill glass, and stir well. Decorate with Slice of Orange, Lemon and a Cherry. Serve with straws.

LEMONADE
[Claret]

Juice 1 Lemon
2 Teaspoons Powdered Sugar
Fill 12 oz. Tom Collins glass with shaved Ice. Add enough water to fill glass, leaving room to float 2 oz. Claret. Decorate with a slice of Orange, Lemon and a Cherry. Serve with straws.

LEMONADE
[Egg]

Juice of 1 Lemon
2 Teaspoons Powdered Sugar
1 Whole Egg
Shake well and strain into 12 oz. Tom Collins glass filled with shaved Ice. Add enough water to fill glass. Serve with straws.

LEMONADE
[Fruit]

Juice 1 Lemon
2 Teaspoons Powdered Sugar
1 oz. Raspberry Syrup
Fill 12 oz. Tom Collins glass with shaved Ice. Add enough water to fill glass and stir well. Decorate with a slice of Orange, Lemon and a Cherry. Serve with straws.

Juice 1 Lemon
2 Teaspoons Powdered Sugar
Yolk 1 Egg
6 oz. Water
Shake well with cracked Ice and strain
into 12 oz. Tom Collins glass. Decorate
with a slice of Orange, Lemon and a
Cherry.

LEMONADE
[Golden]

2 Teaspoons Powdered Sugar
1½ oz. Sherry Wine
1 oz. Sloe Gin
Cut Lemon in quarters and muddle
well with Sugar. Add Sherry and Sloe
Gin. Shake well with cracked Ice and
strain into 12 oz. Tom Collins glass.
Fill glass with Carbonated Water.

LEMONADE
[Modern]

Juice 1 Lemon
2 Teaspoons Powdered Sugar
Fill 12 oz. Tom Collins glass with
shaved Ice. Add enough water to fill
glass and stir well. Decorate with a
slice of Orange, Lemon and a Cherry.
Serve with straws.

LEMONADE
[Plain]

¾ oz. Imported Rum
1½ oz. Applejack
¼ Teaspoon Simple Syrup
Stir well with cracked Ice and strain
into 3 oz. Cocktail glass.

LIBERTY
COCKTAIL

Juice 3 Limes
3 Teaspoons Powdered Sugar
Fill 12 oz. Tom Collins glass with
shaved ice. Add enough water to fill
glass. Stir well and drop Lime in glass.
Add a Cherry. Serve with straws.

LIMEADE

LINSTEAD COCKTAIL	1 oz. Rye or Bourbon Whiskey 1 oz. Pineapple Juice ½ Teaspoon Powdered Sugar ¼ Teaspoon Absinthe Substitute ¼ Teaspoon Lemon Juice Shake well with cracked Ice and strain into 3 oz. Cocktail glass.
LITTLE DEVIL COCKTAIL	Juice of ¼ Lemon ¼ oz. Triple Sec ¾ oz. Imported Rum ¾ oz. Dry Gin Shake well with cracked Ice and strain into 3 oz. Cocktail glass.
LITTLE PRINCESS COCKTAIL	1¼ oz. Italian Vermouth 1¼ oz. Imported Rum Stir well with cracked Ice and strain into 3 oz. Cocktail glass.
LONDON BUCK HIGHBALL	1 Cube of Ice 2 oz. Dry Gin Juice of ½ Lemon Fill 8 oz. Highball glass with Ginger Ale and stir gently.
LONDON COCKTAIL	2 oz. Dry Gin 2 Dashes Orange Bitters ½ Teaspoon Simple Syrup ½ Teaspoon Maraschino Stir well with cracked Ice and strain into 3 oz. Cocktail glass. Add twist of Lemon Peel and drop in glass.
LONDON SPECIAL COCKTAIL	Put Rind of ½ an Orange into 6 oz. Champagne Glass. Add: 1 Lump of Sugar 2 Dashes Bitters Fill with Champagne, well chilled, and stir gently.

¾ oz. Italian Vermouth
1½ oz. Dry Gin
Shake well with cracked Ice and strain
into 3 oz. Cocktail glass.

LONE TREE COCKTAIL

Into 12 oz. Tom Collins glass, put:
½ Teaspoon Powdered Sugar
2 oz. Carbonated Water, and stir.
   Fill glass with cracked Ice and add:
2 oz. Dry Gin
½ oz. French Vermouth.
   Fill with Carbonated Water or
   Ginger Ale.
Insert spiral of Orange or Lemon Peel
(or both) and dangle end over rim of
glass.

LONE TREE COOLER

Juice of ½ Lemon
1 Teaspoon Powdered Sugar
1 Egg
¼ Teaspoon Italian Vermouth
1½ oz. Rye or Bourbon Whiskey
Shake well with cracked Ice and strain
into 4 oz. Cocktail glass.

LOS ANGELES COCKTAIL

2 oz. Sloe Gin
   White of 1 Egg
½ Teaspoon Lemon Juice
½ Teaspoon Raspberry Juice
Shake well with cracked Ice and strain
into 4 oz. Cocktail glass.

LOVE COCKTAIL

93

LOVING CUP

Use large Glass Pitcher.
4 Teaspoons Powdered Sugar
6 oz. Carbonated Water
½ oz. Triple Sec
½ oz. Curacao
2 oz. Brandy
Fill Pitcher with cubes of Ice. Add 1
Pint Claret. Stir well and decorate
with as many Fruits as available and
also Rind of Cucumber inserted on
each side of Pitcher. Top with small
bunch of Mint Sprigs.

**LUXURY
COCKTAIL**

3 oz. Brandy
2 Dashes Orange Bitters
3 oz. well chilled Champagne
Use 6 oz. Saucer Champagne glass.

**MACARONI
COCKTAIL**

¾ oz. Italian Vermouth
1½ oz. Absinthe Substitute
Shake well with cracked Ice and strain
into 3 oz. Cocktail glass.

**MAGNOLIA
BLOSSOM
COCKTAIL**

Juice of ¼ Lemon
½ oz. Sweet Cream
1 oz. Dry Gin
¼ Teaspoon Grenadine
Shake well with cracked Ice and strain
into 3 oz. Cocktail glass.

**MAIDEN'S BLUSH
COCKTAIL No. 1**

¼ Teaspoon Lemon Juice
1 Teaspoon Curacao
1 Teaspoon Grenadine
1½ oz. Dry Gin
Shake well with cracked Ice and strain
into 3 oz. Cocktail glass.

**MAIDEN'S BLUSH
COCKTAIL No. 2.**

¾ oz. Absinthe Substitute
1½ oz. Dry Gin
1 Teaspoon Grenadine
Stir well with cracked Ice and strain
into 3 oz. Cocktail glass.

¼ Teaspoon Orange Juice
¼ Teaspoon Lemon Juice
¼ Teaspoon Triple Sec
2 oz. Dry Gin
Shake well with cracked Ice and strain into 3 oz. Cocktail glass.

MAIDEN'S PRAYER COCKTAIL

¾ oz. Dry Gin
¾ oz. Triple Sec
¾ oz. Grape Juice
Shake well with cracked Ice and strain into 3 oz. Cocktail glass.

MAINBRACE COCKTAIL

¼ oz. Lime Juice
¼ oz. Lemon Juice
½ Teaspoon Powdered Sugar
12 Mint Leaves
Muddle well and pour into 12 oz. Tom Collins glass filled with shaved Ice, and add: 2 oz. Dry Gin. Stir gently, until glass is frosted. Decorate with Sprig of Mint and serve with straws.

MAJOR BAILEY

Juice ½ Lime
2 Cubes of Ice
2 oz. Scotch Whiskey
1 Dash Bitters
Fill 12 oz. Tom Collins glass with Carbonated Water and stir gently.

MAMIE GILROY

Juice ½ Lime
2 Cubes of Ice
2 oz. Scotch Whiskey
Fill 12 oz. Tom Collins glass with Ginger Ale and stir gently.

MAMIE TAYLOR

Juice 1 Lime, drop Skin in glass
2 Cubes of Ice
2 oz. Dry Gin
Fill 12 oz. Tom Collins glass with Ginger Ale and stir gently.

MAMIE'S SISTER

**MANHATTAN
COCKTAIL**

1 Dash Bitters
¾ oz. Italian Vermouth
1½ oz. Rye or Bourbon Whiskey
Stir well with cracked Ice and strain
into 3 oz. Cocktail glass. Serve with a
Cherry.

**MANHATTAN
COCKTAIL [Dry]**

1 Dash Bitters
¾ oz. French Vermouth
1½ oz. Rye or Bourbon Whiskey
Stir well with cracked Ice and strain
into 3 oz. Cocktail glass. Serve with an
Olive.

**MANHATTAN
COCKTAIL
[Sweet]**

1 Dash Bitters
¼ Teaspoon Powdered Sugar
¾ oz. Italian Vermouth
1½ oz. Rye or Bourbon Whiskey
Stir well with cracked Ice and strain
into 3 oz. Cocktail glass. Serve with a
Cherry.

MANILA FIZZ

2 oz. Dry Gin
1 Egg
1 Teaspoon Powdered Sugar
2 oz. Sarsaparilla
Juice 1 Lime or ½ Lemon
Shake well with cracked Ice and strain
into 10 oz. Pilsner glass.

**MARGUERITE
COCKTAIL**

1 Dash Orange Bitters
¾ oz. French Vermouth
¼ Teaspoon Curacao
1½ oz. Dry Gin
Stir well with cracked Ice and strain
into 3 oz. Cocktail glass. Serve with an
Olive.

1 Dash Orange Bitters
1 oz. French Vermouth
¼ Teaspoon Curacao
1 oz. Dry Gin
Shake well with cracked Ice and strain into 3 oz. Cocktail glass. Serve with a Cherry.

MARTINEZ COCKTAIL

1½ oz. Dry Gin
¾ oz. French Vermouth
1 Dash Orange Bitters
Stir well with cracked Ice and strain into 3 oz. Cocktail glass. Serve with an Olive.

MARTINI COCKTAIL [Dry]

1½ oz. Orange Flavored Gin
¾ oz. French Vermouth
Stir well with cracked Ice and strain into 3 oz. Cocktail glass. Serve with an Olive.

MARTINI COCKTAIL [Golden]

1 Dash Orange Bitters
½ oz. French Vermouth
½ oz. Italian Vermouth
1½ oz. Dry Gin
Stir well with cracked Ice and strain into 3 oz. Cocktail glass. Serve with an Olive.

MARTINI COCKTAIL [Medium]

1 Dash Orange Bitters
¾ oz. Italian Vermouth
1½ oz. Dry Gin
Stir well with cracked Ice and strain into 3 oz. Cocktail glass. Serve with a Cherry.

MARTINI COCKTAIL [Sweet]

1½ oz. Dubonnet
¾ oz. French Vermouth
Stir well with cracked Ice and strain into 3 oz. Cocktail glass.

MARY GARDEN COCKTAIL

MARY PICKFORD COCKTAIL

1 oz. Imported Rum
1 oz. Pineapple Juice
¼ Teaspoon Grenadine
¼ Teaspoon Maraschino
Shake well with cracked Ice and strain into 3 oz. Cocktail glass.

MAURICE COCKTAIL

Juice of ¼ Orange
½ oz. Italian Vermouth
½ oz. French Vermouth
1 oz. Dry Gin
1 Dash Bitters
Shake well with cracked Ice and strain into 4 oz. Cocktail glass.

MAY BLOSSOM FIZZ

1 Teaspoon Grenadine
Juice ½ Lemon
2 oz. Swedish Punch
Shake well with cracked Ice and strain into 7 oz. Highball glass. Fill with Carbonated Water.

MAYFAIR COCKTAIL

½ oz. Apricot Flavored Brandy
½ oz. Orange Juice
1 oz. Dry Gin
¼ Teaspoon Clove Syrup
Shake well with cracked Ice and strain into 3 oz. Cocktail glass.

McCLELLAND COCKTAIL

¾ oz. Curacao
1½ oz. Sloe Gin
1 Dash Orange Bitters
Shake well with cracked Ice and strain into 3 oz. Cocktail glass.

MELON COCKTAIL

2 oz. Dry Gin
¼ Teaspoon Lemon Juice
¼ Teaspoon Maraschino
Shake well with cracked Ice and strain into 3 oz. Cocktail glass. Serve with a Cherry.

1¼ oz. Dry Gin
1¼ oz. French Vermouth
½ Teaspoon Benedictine
½ Teaspoon Absinthe Substitute
1 Dash Orange Bitters
Stir well with cracked Ice and strain
into 3 oz. Cocktail glass. Add Twist of
Lemon Peel and drop in glass.

**MERRY WIDOW
COCKTAIL No. 1**

1¼ oz. Maraschino
1¼ oz. Wild Cherry Flavored Brandy
Stir well with cracked Ice and strain
into 3 oz. Cocktail glass. Serve with a
Cherry.

**MERRY WIDOW
COCKTAIL No. 2**

Juice ½ Orange
Juice ½ Lemon
White of 1 Egg
1 Teaspoon Powdered Sugar
1½ oz. Sloe Gin
Shake well with cracked Ice and strain
into 8 oz. Highball glass. Fill with
Carbonated Water.

**MERRY WIDOW
FIZZ**

1¼ oz. Brandy
1¼ oz. Italian Vermouth
½ Teaspoon Simple Syrup
1 Dash Bitters
Stir well with cracked Ice and strain
into 3 oz. Cocktail glass.

**METROPOLITAN
COCKTAIL**

¾ oz. Scotch Whiskey
¾ oz. French Vermouth
¾ oz. Grapefruit Juice
Stir well with cracked Ice and strain
into 3 oz. Cocktail glass.

**MIAMI BEACH
COCKTAIL**

1 oz. Apricot Flavored Brandy
½ oz. Curacao
½ oz. Lemon Juice
Shake well with cracked Ice and strain
into 3 oz. Cocktail glass.

**MIDNIGHT
COCKTAIL**

99

MIKADO COCKTAIL	2 oz. Brandy 2 Dashes Bitters ½ Teaspoon Creme de Cacao ½ Teaspoon Curacao Shake well with cracked Ice and strain into 3 oz. Cocktail glass.

MILK PUNCH	1 Teaspoon Powdered Sugar 2 oz. Rye or Bourbon Whiskey ½ pt. Milk Shake well with cracked Ice and strain into 12 oz. Tom Collins glass. Grate Nutmeg on top.

MILLIONAIRE COCKTAIL	White of 1 Egg ¼ Teaspoon Grenadine ½ oz. Curacao 1½ oz. Rye or Bourbon Whiskey Shake well with cracked Ice and strain into 4 oz. Cocktail glass.

MILLION DOLLAR COCKTAIL	2 Teaspoons Pineapple Juice 1 Teaspoon Grenadine White of 1 Egg ¾ oz. Italian Vermouth 1½ oz. Dry Gin Shake well with cracked Ice and strain into 4 oz. Cocktail glass.

MINNEHAHA COCKTAIL	Juice of ¼ Orange ½ oz. French Vermouth ½ oz. Italian Vermouth 1 oz. Dry Gin Shake well with cracked Ice and strain into 4 oz. Cocktail glass.

MINT COCKTAIL

Juice ½ Lemon
1 Teaspoon Powdered Sugar
2 oz. Mint Flavored Gin
Pour into 12 oz. Tom Collins glass. Add several Cubes of Ice, fill with Carbonated Water and stir well. Decorate with slice of Lemon, Orange and a Cherry. Serve with straws.

MINT HIGHBALL

1 Cube of Ice
2 oz. Creme de Menthe
Fill 8 oz. Highball glass with Ginger Ale or Carbonated Water. Add twist of Lemon Peel, if desired, and stir gently.

MINT JULEP

Into Silver Mug or 12 oz. Tom Collins glass put:
4 Sprigs of Mint
1 Teaspoon Powdered Sugar
2 Teaspoons of Water, and muddle. Fill glass or mug with shaved Ice, add 2½ oz. Straight Bourbon Whiskey, and stir gently until glass is frosted. Decorate with slice of Orange, Lemon, Pineapple and a Cherry. Insert 5 or 6 Sprigs of Mint on top. Serve with straws.

MINT JULEP
[Southern Style]

Fill silver mug or 12 oz. Tom Collins glass with finely shaved Ice. Add 2½ oz. Bourbon Whiskey and stir until glass is heavily frosted. (Do not hold glass with hand while stirring.) Add 1 Teaspoon Powdered Sugar and fill balance with water, and stir. Decorate with 5 or 6 Sprigs of Fresh Mint so that the tops are about 2 inches above rim of mug or glass. Use short straws so that it is necessary to bury nose in Mint. The Mint is intended for odor rather than taste.

**MR. MANHATTAN
COCKTAIL**

Muddle Lump of Sugar and
4 Sprigs of Mint
¼ Teaspoons Lemon Juice
1 Teaspoon Orange Juice
1½ oz. Dry Gin
Shake well with cracked Ice and strain
into 3 oz. Cocktail glass.

**MODERN
COCKTAIL**

1½ oz. Scotch Whiskey
½ Teaspoon Lemon Juice
¼ Teaspoon Absinthe Substitute
½ Teaspoon Jamaica Rum
1 Dash Orange Bitters
Shake well with cracked Ice and strain
into 3 oz. Cocktail glass. Serve with a
Cherry.

**MONTE CARLO
IMPERIAL
HIGHBALL**

2 oz. Dry Gin
½ oz. Creme de Menthe (White)
Juice ¼ Lemon
Shake well with cracked Ice and strain
into 8 oz. Highball glass and fill glass
with Champagne.

**MONTMARTRE
COCKTAIL**

1¼ oz. Dry Gin
½ oz. Italian Vermouth
½ oz. Triple Sec
Stir well with cracked Ice and strain
into 3 oz. Cocktail glass. Serve with a
Cherry.

**MORNING
COCKTAIL**

1 oz. Brandy
1 oz. French Vermouth
¼ Teaspoon Curacao
¼ Teaspoon Maraschino
¼ Teaspoon Absinthe Substitute
2 Dashes Orange bitters
Stir well with cracked Ice and strain
into 3 oz. Cocktail glass. Serve with a
Cherry.

Juice ½ Lemon or 1 Lime
1 Teaspoon Powdered Sugar
White of 1 Egg
½ Teaspoon Absinthe Substitute
2 oz. Scotch Whiskey
Shake well with cracked Ice and strain into 8 oz. Highball glass. Fill with Carbonated Water.

½ oz. Lemon Juice
¾ oz. Imported Rum
¾ oz. Triple Sec
½ oz. Grenadine
Shake well with cracked Ice and strain into 3 oz. Cocktail glass.

1½ oz. Sloe Gin
¾ oz. Italian Vermouth
1 Dash Bitters
Stir well with cracked Ice and strain into 3 oz. Cocktail glass.

White of 1 Egg
¼ Teaspoon Lemon Juice
¼ Teaspoon French Vermouth
¼ Teaspoon Italian Vermouth
1½ oz. Rye or Bourbon Whiskey
Shake well with cracked Ice and strain into 4 oz. Cocktail glass.

Into a Metal Mug, put:
1 Lump of Sugar
Juice ½ Lemon
1 Dash Bitters
1 Teaspoon Mixed Cinnamon and Nutmeg
5 oz. Claret
Heat poker red hot and hold in liquid until boiling and serve.

NAPOLEON COCKTAIL

2 oz. Dry Gin
½ Teaspoon Curacao
½ Teaspoon Dubonnet
Stir well with cracked Ice and strain into 3 oz. Cocktail glass.

NEVADA COCKTAIL

1½ oz. Imported Rum
1 oz. Grapefruit Juice
Juice of 1 Lime
1 Dash Bitters
3 Teaspoons Powdered Sugar
Shake well with cracked Ice and strain into 4 oz. Cocktail glass.

NEWBURY COCKTAIL

1 oz. Italian Vermouth
1 oz. Dry Gin
Twist of Lemon Peel
1 Teaspoon Curacao
Shake well with cracked Ice and strain into 3 oz. Cocktail glass. Twist of Orange Peel and drop in glass.

NEW ORLEANS GIN FIZZ

Juice ½ Lemon
1 Teaspoon Powdered Sugar
White of 1 Egg
2 oz. Dry Gin
1 Tablespoon Sweet Cream
½ Teaspoon Orange Flower Water
Shake extra well with cracked Ice and strain into 12 oz. Tom Collins glass. Fill with Carbonated Water.

NEW YORK COCKTAIL

Juice 1 Lime or ½ Lemon
1 Teaspoon Powdered Sugar
1½ oz. Rye or Bourbon Whiskey
½ Teaspoon Grenadine
Twist of Orange Peel
Shake well with cracked Ice and strain into 3 oz. Cocktail glass. Add twist of Lemon Peel and drop in glass.

Juice ½ Lemon
1 Teaspoon Powdered Sugar
2 oz. Rye or Bourbon Whiskey
Shake well with cracked Ice and strain
into 6 oz. Sour glass, leaving about ½
inch in which to float Claret. Decorate
with a half-slice of Lemon and a
Cherry.

2 oz. Imported Rum
1 Teaspoon Powdered Sugar
Add enough Warm Milk to fill a Tom &
Jerry Mug. Grate a little Nutmeg on
top.

White of 1 Egg
½ oz. Lemon Juice
½ oz. Maraschino
1 oz. Dry Gin
Shake well with cracked Ice and strain
into 4 oz. Cocktail glass and top with
Whipped Cream.

Use Old Fashioned Cocktail glass.
½ Lump of Sugar
2 Dashes Bitters
   Add enough Water to cover Sugar
   and muddle well.
1 Cube of Ice
2 oz. Rye or Bourbon Whiskey
Stir well. Add Twist of Lemon Rind
and drop in glass. Decorate with Slice
of Orange, Lemon and a Cherry. Serve
with stirring rod.

⅓ Creme de Cacao
⅓ Blackberry Flavored Brandy
⅓ Wild Cherry Flavored Brandy
Pour carefully, in order given, into
Pousse Cafe glass so that each
ingredient floats on preceding one.

OLD MR. COTTON SPECIAL COCKTAIL No. 1

1½ oz. Dry Gin
¼ Teaspoon Powdered Sugar
1 Teaspoon Orange Juice
1 Teaspoon Creme de Cacao
1 Teaspoon Italian Vermouth
   Twist of Lemon Peel
Shake well with cracked Ice and strain into 3 oz. Cocktail glass.

OLD MR. COTTON SPECIAL COCKTAIL No. 2

1½ oz. Rye or Bourbon Whiskey
¾ oz. Port Wine
1 Teaspoon Italian Vermouth
2 Dashes Bitters
Stir well with cracked Ice and strain into 3 oz. Cocktail glass.

OLD PAL COCKTAIL

½ oz. Grenadine
½ oz. Italian Vermouth
1¼ oz. Rye or Bourbon Whiskey
Stir well with cracked Ice and strain into 3 oz. Cocktail glass.

OLYMPIC COCKTAIL

¾ oz. Orange Juice
¾ oz. Curacao
¾ oz. Brandy
Shake well with cracked Ice and strain into 3 oz. Cocktail glass.

OPAL COCKTAIL

1 oz. Dry Gin
½ oz. Orange Juice
½ oz. Triple Sec
¼ Teaspoon Powdered Sugar
½ Teaspoon Orange Flower Water
Shake well with cracked Ice and strain into 3 oz. Cocktail glass.

½ oz. Grenadine
½ oz. Italian Vermouth
1¼ oz. Rye or Bourbon Whiskey
Stir well with cracked Ice and strain
into 3 oz. Cocktail glass.

½ oz. Maraschino
½ oz. Dubonnet
1½ oz. Dry Gin
Stir well with cracked Ice and strain
into 3 oz. Cocktail glass.

OPERA COCKTAIL

Juice 2 Oranges
1 Teaspoon Powdered Sugar
Add 2 Cubes of Ice and enough Water
to fill 12 oz. Tom Collins glass and stir
well. Decorate with a slice of Orange,
Lemon and 2 Cherries. Serve with
straws.

ORANGEADE

½ oz. Italian Vermouth
½ oz. Triple Sec
1½ oz. Dry Gin
Stir well with cracked Ice and strain
into 3 oz. Cocktail glass. Serve with a
Cherry.

**ORANGE BLOOM
COCKTAIL**

1 oz. Dry Gin
1 oz. Orange Juice
¼ Teaspoon Powdered Sugar
Shake well with cracked Ice and strain
into 3 oz. Cocktail glass.

**ORANGE
BLOSSOM
COCKTAIL**

Juice ½ Lemon
1 Teaspoon Powdered Sugar
2 oz. Orange Flavored Gin
Pour into 12 oz. Tom Collins glass. Add
several Cubes of Ice, fill with
Carbonated Water and stir well.
Decorate with slice of Lemon, Orange
and a Cherry. Serve with straws.

**ORANGE GIN
COLLINS**

ORANGE GIN FIZZ

Juice ½ Lemon
1 Teaspoon Powdered Sugar
2 oz. Orange Flavored Gin
Shake well with cracked Ice and strain into 7 oz. Highball glass. Fill with Carbonated Water.

ORANGE GIN HIGHBALL

1 Cube of Ice
2 oz. Orange Flavored Gin
Fill 8 oz. Highball glass with Ginger Ale or Carbonated Water. Add twist of Lemon Peel, if desired, and stir gently.

ORANGE GIN RICKEY

1 Cube of Ice
Juice ½ Lime
2 oz. Orange Flavored Gin
Fill 8 oz. Highball glass with Carbonated Water and stir. Leave Lime in glass.

ORANGE MILK FIZZ

Juice ½ Lemon
1 Teaspoon Powdered Sugar
2 oz. Orange Flavored Gin
2 oz. Milk
Shake well with cracked Ice and strain into 8 oz. Highball glass. Fill with Carbonated Water.

ORANGE SMILE

1 Egg
Juice 1 Large Orange
1 Tablespoon Raspberry Syrup or Grenadine
Shake well with cracked Ice and strain into 8 oz. Stem Goblet.

108

1 oz. Rye or Bourbon Whiskey
½ oz. Italian Vermouth
½ oz. Curacao
Juice of ½ Lime
Shake well with cracked Ice and strain
into 3 oz. Cocktail glass.

ORIENTAL COCKTAIL

1¼ oz. Irish Whiskey
1¼ oz. Italian Vermouth
1 Dash Bitters
Stir well with cracked Ice and strain
into 3 oz. Cocktail glass.

PADDY COCKTAIL

¾ oz. Italian Vermouth
¾ oz. French Vermouth
¾ oz. Dry Gin
1 Dash Orange Bitters
1 Teaspoon Creme de Menthe
(White)
Stir well with cracked Ice and strain
into 3 oz. Cocktail glass.

PALL MALL COCKTAIL

1½ oz. Dry Gin
¼ oz. Italian Vermouth
¼ oz. Grapefruit Juice
Shake well with cracked Ice and strain
into 3 oz. Cocktail glass.

PALM BEACH COCKTAIL

2 oz. Rye or Bourbon Whiskey
1 Dash Bitters
½ Teaspoon Lemon Juice
Stir well with cracked Ice and strain
into 3 oz. Cocktail glass.

PALMER COCKTAIL

1¼ oz. Imported Rum
1¼ oz. French Vermouth
2 Dashes Bitters
Stir well with cracked Ice and strain
into 3 oz. Cocktail glass.

PALMETTO COCKTAIL

PANAMA COCKTAIL	1 oz. Creme de Cacao 1 oz. Sweet Cream 1 oz. Brandy Shake well with cracked Ice and strain into 4 oz. Cocktail glass.
PARADISE COCKTAIL	1 oz. Apricot Flavored Brandy ¾ oz. Dry Gin Juice ¼ Orange Shake well with cracked Ice and strain into 3 oz. Cocktail glass.
PARISIAN BLONDE COCKTAIL	¾ oz. Sweet Cream ¾ oz. Curacao ¾ oz. Jamaica Rum Shake well with cracked Ice and strain into 3 oz. Cocktail glass.
PASSION DAIQUIRI COCKTAIL	1½ oz. Imported Rum Juice 1 Lime 1 Teaspoon Powdered Sugar ½ oz. Passion Fruit Shake well with cracked Ice and strain into 3 oz. Cocktail glass.
PEACH BLOSSOM	1 Teaspoon Lemon Juice ½ Teaspoon Powdered Sugar 2 oz. Dry Gin ½ Peach Shake well with cracked Ice and strain into 8 oz. Highball glass. Fill with Carbonated Water.
PEACH BLOW FIZZ	Juice ½ Lemon White of 1 Egg 2 Teaspoons Grenadine ½ Teaspoon Powdered Sugar 1 oz. Sweet Cream 2 oz. Dry Gin Shake well with cracked Ice and strain into 10 oz. Highball glass. Fill with Carbonated Water.

1½ oz. Peach Flavored Brandy
½ Teaspoon Powdered Sugar
Shake well with cracked Ice and strain into 3 oz. Cocktail glass, leaving enough room on which to float a Tablespoon of Port Wine.

PEACH SANGAREE

¾ oz. French Vermouth
1½ oz. Dry Gin
¼ Teaspoon Absinthe Substitute
¼ Teaspoon Dubonnet
Stir well with cracked Ice and strain into 3 oz. Cocktail glass.

PEGGY COCKTAIL

Muddle Lump of Sugar with 1 Teaspoon of Water, in 6 oz. Sour glass. Fill with finely shaved Ice, add 2 oz. Rye or Bourbon Whiskey and stir well. Decorate with 2 slices of Lemon.

PENDENNIS TODDY

¼ oz. French Vermouth
¼ oz. Italian Vermouth
1½ oz. Dry Gin
1 Dash Bitters
Stir well with cracked Ice and strain into 3 oz. Cocktail glass.

PERFECT COCKTAIL

2 Dashes Bitters
¾ oz. Orange Juice
¾ oz. French Vermouth
¾ oz. Dry Gin
Shake well with cracked Ice and strain into 3 oz. Cocktail glass.

PETER PAN COCKTAIL

1¼ oz. Dubonnet
1¼ oz. Brandy
¼ Teaspoon Absinthe Substitute
Stir well with cracked Ice and strain into 3 oz. Cocktail glass.

PHOEBE SNOW COCKTAIL

PICCADILLY
COCKTAIL

¾ oz. French Vermouth
1½ oz. Dry Gin
¼ Teaspoon Absinthe Substitute
¼ Teaspoon Grenadine
Shake well with cracked Ice and strain
into 3 oz. Cocktail glass.

PIKE'S PEAK
COOLER

Juice ½ Lemon
1 Teaspoon Powdered Sugar
1 Egg
Shake well with cracked Ice and strain
into 12 oz. Tom Collins glass and fill
with Hard Cider.
Insert Spiral of Orange or Lemon Peel
(or both) and dangle end over rim of
glass.

PINEAPPLE
COCKTAIL

¾ oz. Pineapple Juice
1½ oz. Imported Rum
½ Teaspoon Lemon Juice
Shake well with cracked Ice and strain
into 3 oz. Cocktail glass.

PINEAPPLE
COOLER

Into 12 oz. Tom Collins glass, put:
½ Teaspoon Powdered Sugar
2 oz. Carbonated Water, and stir.
Fill glass with cracked Ice and add:
2 oz. Dry White Wine.
Fill with Carbonated Water.
Insert Spiral of Orange or Lemon Peel
(or both) and dangle end over rim of
glass.

½ oz. Pineapple Juice
Juice ½ Lime
1 oz. Imported Rum
Shake well with cracked Ice and strain
into 3 oz. Cocktail glass.

**PINEAPPLE
DREAM COCKTAIL**

1 oz. Pineapple Juice
½ Teaspoon Powdered Sugar
2 oz. Imported Rum
Shake well with cracked Ice and strain
into 7 oz. Highball glass. Fill with
Carbonated Water.

**PINEAPPLE
FIZZ**

Juice of ¼ Lemon
White of 1 Egg
1 oz. Sloe Gin
1 oz. Creme de Yvette
Shake well with cracked Ice and strain
into 4 oz. Cocktail glass.

**PING-PONG
COCKTAIL**

see GIN AND BITTERS

PINK GIN

White of 1 Egg
1 Teaspoon Grenadine
1 Teaspoon Sweet Cream
1½ oz. Dry Gin
Shake well with cracked Ice and strain
into 4 oz. Cocktail glass.

**PINK LADY
COCKTAIL**

Juice ¼ Lemon
White of 1 Egg
¾ oz. Apricot Nectar
¾ oz. Rye or Bourbon Whiskey
Shake well with cracked Ice and strain
into 3 oz. Cocktail glass.

**PINK PUFF
COCKTAIL**

113

PINK ROSE **FIZZ**	Juice ½ Lemon 1 Teaspoon Powdered Sugar White of 1 Egg ½ Teaspoon Grenadine 2 Teaspoons Sweet Cream 2 oz. Dry Gin Shake well with cracked Ice and strain into 8 oz. Highball glass. Fill with Carbonated Water.
PINK WHISKERS **COCKTAIL**	¾ oz. Apricot Flavored Brandy ¾ oz. French Vermouth 1 oz. Orange Juice 1 Teaspoon Grenadine ¼ Teaspoon Creme de Menthe (White) Shake well with cracked Ice and strain into 4 oz. Cocktail glass and top with a little Port Wine.
PLAIN **VERMOUTH** **COCKTAIL**	See VERMOUTH COCKTAIL
PLANTER'S **COCKTAIL**	Juice of ¼ Lemon ½ Teaspoon Powdered Sugar 1½ oz. Jamaica Rum Shake well with cracked Ice and strain into 3 oz. Cocktail glass.
PLANTER'S **PUNCH No. 1**	Juice 2 Limes 2 Teaspoons Powdered Sugar 2 oz. Carbonated Water Fill 12 oz. Tom Collins glass with shaved Ice and stir until glass is frosted. Add 2 Dashes Bitters. 2½ oz. Imported Rum. Stir and decorate with slice of Lemon, Orange, Pineapple and a Cherry. Serve with straws.

Juice 1 Lime
Juice ½ Lemon
Juice ½ Orange
1 Teaspoon Pineapple Juice
2 oz. Imported Rum
Pour above into 16 oz. glass, well filled with shaved Ice. Stir until glass is frosted. Then add 1 oz. Jamaica Rum and top with ¼ Teaspoon Curacao. Decorate with slice of Orange, Lemon, Pineapple and a Cherry, also Sprig of Mint dipped in Powdered Sugar. Serve with straws.

PLANTER'S PUNCH No. 2

¾ oz. Italian Vermouth
¾ oz. French Vermouth
¾ Dry Gin
1 Strip of Pineapple
Shake well with cracked Ice and strain into 3 oz. Cocktail glass.

PLAZA COCKTAIL

1¼ oz. Italian Vermouth
1¼ oz. Imported rum
Stir well with cracked Ice and strain into 3 oz. Cocktail glass.

POKER COCKTAIL

Muddle 3 slices of Orange and 3 slices of Pineapple
2 oz. Dry Gin
½ oz. Italian Vermouth
½ Teaspoon Grenadine
Shake well with cracked Ice and strain into 4 oz. Cocktail glass.

POLLYANNA COCKTAIL

½ oz. Lemon Juice
½ oz. Orange Juice
1 oz. Dry Gin
Shake well with cracked Ice and strain into 3 oz. Cocktail glass.

POLO COCKTAIL

POOP DECK COCKTAIL	1¼ oz. Blackberry Flavored Brandy ½ oz. Port Wine ½ oz. Brandy Stir well with cracked Ice and strain into 3 oz. Cocktail glass.
POPPY COCKTAIL	¾ oz. Creme de Cacao 1½ oz. Dry Gin Shake well with cracked Ice and strain into 3 oz. Cocktail glass.
PORT AND STARBOARD	½ oz. Grenadine ½ oz. Green Creme de Menthe Pour carefully, in order given, into Pousse Cafe glass, so that each ingredient floats on preceding one.
PORT MILK PUNCH	1 Teaspoon Powdered Sugar 3 oz. Port Wine ½ pt. Milk Shake well with cracked Ice, strain into 12 oz. Tom Collins glass and grate Nutmeg on top.
PORT WINE COBBLER	1 Teaspoon Powdered Sugar 2 oz. Carbonated Water Fill 10 oz. Goblet with shaved Ice Add 3 oz. Port Wine Stir well and decorate with fruits in season. Serve with straws.
PORT WINE COCKTAIL	2¼ oz. Port Wine ½ Teaspoon Brandy Stir slightly with cracked Ice and strain into 3 oz. Cocktail glass.

1 Egg
1 Teaspoon Powdered Sugar
3 oz. Port Wine
  Fill glass with Milk
Shake well with cracked Ice and strain
into 12 oz. Tom Collins glass. Grate
Nutmeg on top.

**PORT WINE
EGG NOG**

  1 Egg
  1 Teaspoon Powdered Sugar
1½ oz. Port Wine
  2 Teaspoons Sweet Cream
    (if desired)
Shake well with cracked Ice and
strain into 5 oz. Flip glass. Grate a
little Nutmeg on top.

PORT WINE FLIP

½ Lump Sugar
2 oz. Port Wine
Fill Hot Whiskey Glass with hot
Water and stir. Grate Nutmeg on top.

**PORT WINE
NEGUS**

1½ oz. Port Wine
  1 Teaspoon Powdered Sugar
Shake well with cracked Ice and strain
into 3 oz. Cocktail glass, leaving
enough room in which to float a
tablespoon of Brandy.

**PORT WINE
SANGAREE**

  1 Cube of Ice
    Juice ½ Lime
1½ oz. Dry Gin
½ Teaspoon Raspberry Syrup
Fill 8 oz. Highball glass with
Carbonated Water and stir. Leave
Lime in glass.

**PORTO RICO
RICKEY**

117

POUSSE CAFE

1/6 Grenadine
1/6 Yellow Chartreuse
1/6 Creme de Yvette •
1/6 Creme de Menthe (White)
1/6 Green Chartreuse
1/6 Brandy
Pour carefully, in order given, into Pousse Cafe glass so that each ingredient floats on preceding one.
See Index on page 14 for complete list of Pousee Cafe recipes.

POUSSE L'AMOUR

⅓ oz. Maraschino
   Yolk of 1 Egg
⅓ oz. Benedictine
⅓ oz. Brandy
Pour carefully, in order given, into 2 oz. Sherry glass, so that each ingredient floats on preceding one.

**PRAIRIE HEN
COCKTAIL**

1 Whole Egg
1 Teaspoon Worcestershire Sauce
½ Teaspoon Vinegar
1 Drop Tobasco Sauce
   Season with a little Salt and Pepper
Use 5 oz. Delmonico glass.

**PRAIRIE OYSTER
COCKTAIL**

1 Whole Egg
1 Teaspoon Worcestershire Sauce
1 Teaspoon Tomato Catsup
½ Teaspoon Vinegar
   Pinch of Pepper
1 Drop Tabasco Sauce
Use 5 oz. Delmonico glass.

**PREAKNESS
COCKTAIL**

¾ oz. Italian Vermouth
1½ oz. Rye or Bourbon Whiskey
1 Dash Bitters
½ Teaspoon Benedictine
Shake well with cracked Ice and strain into 3 oz. Cocktail Glass. Add Twist of Lemon Peel and drop in glass.

½ oz. Orange Juice
½ oz. Italian Vermouth
1¼ oz. Brandy
¼ Teaspoon Absinthe Substitute
Shake well with cracked Ice and strain
into 3 oz. Cocktail glass.

PRESTO COCKTAIL

¾ Apricot Flavored Brandy
¼ Sweet Cream
Pour Cream carefully on top, so that it
does not mix. Use Pousse Cafe glass.

**PRINCESS POUSSE
CAFE**

½ oz. Apricot Flavored Brandy
½ oz. Applejack
1 oz. Dry Gin
¼ Teaspoon Lemon Juice
Shake well with cracked Ice and strain
into 3 oz. Cocktail glass.

**PRINCE'S SMILE
COCKTAIL**

1 oz. Dry Gin
1 oz. French Vermouth
Juice ½ Lime
Stir well with cracked Ice and strain
into 3 oz. Cocktail glass.

**PRINCETON
COCKTAIL**

See Index on page 14 for complete list
of Punch recipes.

PUNCHES

¾ oz. Imported Rum
¾ oz. Brandy
Juice ¼ Lemon
2 Teaspoons Raspberry Syrup
Shake well with cracked Ice and strain
into 3 oz. Cocktail glass.

**QUAKER'S
COCKTAIL**

¾ oz. Sherry Wine
1½ oz. Imported Rum
Juice ½ Lime
Stir well with cracked Ice and strain
into 3 oz. Cocktail glass.

**QUARTER DECK
COCKTAIL**

119

QUEEN CHARLOTTE	2 oz. Claret 1 oz. Raspberry Syrup or Grenadine Pour into 12 oz. Tom Collins glass. Add cube of Ice, fill with Lemon Soda and stir.
QUEEN ELIZABETH COCKTAIL	1½ oz. Dry Gin ½ oz. French Vermouth ¼ oz. Benedictine Stir well with cracked Ice and strain into 3 oz. Cocktail glass.
RACQUET CLUB COCKTAIL	1½ oz. Dry Gin ¾ oz. French Vermouth 1 Dash Orange Bitters Stir well with cracked Ice and strain into 3 oz. Cocktail glass.
RAMOS FIZZ	Juice ½ Lemon White of 1 Egg 1 Teaspoon Powdered Sugar 2 oz. Dry Gin 1 Tablespoon Sweet Cream ½ Teaspoon Orange Flower Water Shake extra well with cracked Ice and strain into 12 oz. Tom Collins glass. Fill with Carbonated Water.
RATTLESNAKE COCKTAIL	1½ oz. Rye or Bourbon Whiskey White of 1 Egg 1 Teaspoon Lemon Juice ½ Teaspoon Powdered Sugar ¼ Teaspoon Absinthe Substitute Shake well with cracked Ice and strain into 4 oz. Cocktail glass.
RED SWIZZLE	Made same as Gin Swizzle and add 1 Tablespoon of Grenadine. If desired, Rum, Brandy or Whiskey may be substituted for the Gin.

¾ oz. French Vermouth
1½ oz. Sherry Wine
 1 Dash Orange Bitters
Stir well with cracked Ice and strain into 3 oz. Cocktail glass. Serve with a Cherry.

REFORM COCKTAIL

 Into 12 oz. Tom Collins glass, put:
½ Teaspoon Powdered Sugar
2 oz. Carbonated Water, and stir
 Fill glass with Cracked Ice and add:
2 oz. Dry Gin
 Fill with Carbonated Water or Ginger Ale
Insert spiral of Orange or Lemon Peel (or both) and dangle end over rim of glass.

REMSEN COOLER

 Juice ¼ Lemon
½ oz. Apricot Flavored Brandy
 1 oz. Dry Gin
Shake well with cracked Ice and strain into 3 oz. Cocktail glass.

RESOLUTE COCKTAIL

Use Large Glass Pitcher
 4 Teaspoons Powdered Sugar
 6 oz. Carbonated Water
½ oz. Triple Sec
½ oz. Curacao
 2 oz. Brandy
Fill pitcher with cubes of Ice. Add 1 pint of Rhine Wine. Stir well and decorate with as many fruits as available and also Rind of Cucumber inserted on each side of pitcher. Top with small bunch of Mint Sprigs. Serve in 5 oz. Claret glass.

RHINE WINE CUP

See Index on page 14 for complete list of Rickey recipes.

RICKIES

121

ROBERT E. LEE
COOLER

Into 12 oz. Tom Collin glass, put:
Juice ½ Lime
½ Teaspoon Powdered Sugar
2 oz. Carbonated Water, and stir
Fill glass with Cracked Ice and add:
¼ Teaspoon Absinthe Substitute
2 oz. Dry Gin
Fill with Ginger Ale
Insert spiral of Orange or Lemon Peel
(or both) and dangle end over rim of
glass.

ROB ROY
COCKTAIL

¾ oz. Italian Vermouth
1½ oz. Scotch Whiskey
1 Dash Orange Bitters
Stir well with cracked Ice and strain
into 3 oz. Cocktail glass.

ROBSON
COCKTAIL

2 Teaspoons Lemon Juice
½ oz. Orange Juice
¼ oz. Grenadine
1 oz. Jamaica Rum
Shake well with cracked Ice and strain
into 3 oz. Cocktail glass.

ROC-A-COE
COCKTAIL

1¼ oz. Sherry
1¼ oz. Dry Gin
Stir well with cracked Ice and strain
into 3 oz. Cocktail glass. Serve with a
Cherry.

ROLLS ROYCE
COCKTAIL

½ oz. French Vermouth
½ oz. Italian Vermouth
1¼ oz. Dry Gin
¼ Teaspoon Benedictine
Stir well with cracked Ice and strain
into 3 oz. Cocktail glass.

1 oz. Dry Gin
1/2 oz. French Vermouth
1/2 oz. Italian Vermouth
Add 2 or 3 Strawberries. Shake well
with cracked Ice and strain into 3 oz.
Cocktail glass.

ROMA COCKTAIL

3/4 oz. Italian Vermouth
1 1/2 oz. Irish Whiskey
1 Dash Orange bitters
Stir well with cracked Ice and strain
into 3 oz. Cocktail glass.

RORY O'MORE

1/2 oz. Apricot Flavored Brandy
1/2 oz. French Vermouth
1 oz. Dry Gin
1/2 Teaspoon Lemon Juice
1 Teaspoon Grenadine
Shake well with cracked Ice and strain
into 3 oz. Cocktail glass. Frost edge of
glass by rubbing with Lemon and
dipping in Powdered Sugar.

ROSE COCKTAIL
[English]

1/2 oz. Wild Cherry Flavored Brandy
1/2 oz. French Vermouth
1 1/4 oz. Dry Gin
Stir well with cracked Ice and strain
into 3 oz. Cocktail glass.

ROSE COCKTAIL
[French]

3/4 oz. French Vermouth
1 1/2 oz. Dry Gin
1/2 Teaspoon Grenadine
Stir well with cracked Ice and strain
into 3 oz. Cocktail glass. Twist of
Lemon Peel on top and drop in glass.

ROSELYN
COCKTAIL

Juice 1 Lime
1 Tablespoon Grenadine
Yolk 1 Egg
1 1/2 oz. Dry Gin
Shake well with cracked Ice and strain
into 4 oz. Cocktail glass.

ROYAL CLOVER
CLUB COCKTAIL

123

ROYAL COCKTAIL

1 Whole Egg
Juice ½ Lemon
1 Teaspoon Powdered Sugar
1½ oz. Dry Gin
Shake well with cracked Ice and strain
into 4 oz. Cocktail glass.

ROYAL FIZZ

Juice ½ Lemon
1 Teaspoon Powdered Sugar
2 oz. Dry Gin
1 Whole Egg
Shake well with cracked Ice and strain
into 8 oz. Highball glass. Fill with
Carbonated Water.

**ROYAL SMILE
COCKTAIL**

Juice ¼ Lemon
1 Teaspoon Grenadine
½ oz. Dry Gin
1 oz. Applejack
Stir well with cracked Ice and strain
into 3 oz. Cocktail glass.

RUBY FIZZ

Juice ½ Lemon
1 Teaspoon Powdered Sugar
White of 1 Egg
1 Teaspoon Grenadine
2 oz. Sloe Gin
Shake well with cracked Ice and strain
into 8 oz. Highball glass. Fill with
Carbonated Water.

RUM COBBLER

1 Teaspoon Powdered Sugar
2 oz. Carbonated Water
Fill 10 oz. Goblet with Shaved Ice
Add 2 oz. Rum
Stir well and decorate with fruits in
season. Serve with straws.

Juice 1 Lime
1 Teaspoon Powdered Sugar
2 oz. Rum
Pour into 12 oz. Tom Collins glass. Add
several Cubes of Ice, fill with
Carbonated Water and stir well.
Decorate with slice of Lemon and a
Cherry and drop Lime in glass. Serve
with straws.

RUM COLLINS

Into 12 oz. Tom Collins glass, put:
½ Teaspoon Powdered Sugar
2 oz. Carbonated Water, and stir
  Fill glass with Cracked Ice and add:
2 oz. Rum
  Fill with Carbonated Water or
  Ginger Ale
Insert spiral of Orange or Lemon Peel
(or both) and dangle end over rim of
glass.

RUM COOLER

Juice of ½ Lemon
½ Teaspoon Powdered Sugar
1 Teaspoon Raspberry Syrup or
  Grenadine
2 oz. Rum
Shake well with cracked Ice and strain
into Stein or 8 oz. Metal cup. Add Cube
of Ice and decorate with fruit.

RUM DAISY

1 Egg
1 Teaspoon Powdered Sugar
2 oz. Rum
  Fill glass with Milk
Shake well with cracked Ice and strain
into 12 oz. Tom Collins glass. Grate
Nutmeg on top.

RUM EGG NOG

125

RUM FIX

Juice ½ Lemon or 1 Lime
1 Teaspoon Powdered Sugar
1 Teaspoon Water and stir
Fill glass with Shaved Ice
2½ oz. Rum
Use 12 oz. Tom Collins glass. Stir well. Add slice of Lemon. Serve with straws.

RUM HIGHBALL

1 Cube of Ice
2 oz. Rum
Fill 8 oz. Highball glass with Ginger Ale or Carbonated Water. Add twist of Lemon Peel, if desired, and stir gently.

RUM MILK PUNCH

1 Teaspoon Powdered Sugar
2 oz. Rum
½ pt. Milk
Shake well with cracked Ice, strain into 12 oz. Tom Collins glass and grate Nutmeg on top.

RUM RICKEY

1 Cube of Ice
Juice ½ Lime
1½ oz. Imported Rum
Fill 8 oz. Highball glass with Carbonated Water and stir. Leave Lime in glass.

RUM SMASH

Muddle 1 Lump of Sugar with
1 oz. Carbonated Water and
4 Sprigs of Green Mint
Add 2 oz. Rum, then a Cube of Ice Stir and decorate with a slice of Orange and a Cherry, Twist Lemon Peel on top. Use Old Fashioned Cocktail glass.

RUM SOUR

Juice ½ Lemon
½ Teaspoon Powdered Sugar
2 oz. Rum
Shake well with cracked Ice and strain into 6 oz. Sour glass. Fill with Carbonated Water. Decorate with a half-slice of Lemon and a Cherry.

RUM SWIZZLE

Made same as Gin Swizzle, using 2 oz. Rum.

RUM TODDY

Use Old Fashioned Cocktail glass.
½ Teaspoon Powdered Sugar
2 Teaspoons Water
2 oz. Rum
1 Lump of Ice
Stir well and Twist Lemon Peel on top.

RUM TODDY
[Hot]

Put Lump of Sugar into Hot Whiskey glass and fill with two-third Boiling Water. Add 2 oz. Rum. Stir and decorate with slice of Lemon. Grate Nutmeg on top.

RUSSET COCKTAIL

1¼ oz. Sweet Cider
1¼ oz. Dry Gin
½ Teaspoon Grenadine
Stir well with cracked Ice and strain into 3 oz. Cocktail glass.

RUSSIAN COCKTAIL

¾ oz. Creme de Cacao
¾ oz. Dry Gin
¾ oz. Vodka
Shake well with cracked Ice and strain into 3 oz. Cocktail glass.

RYE HIGHBALL

1 Cube of Ice
2 oz. Rye Whiskey
Fill 8 oz. Highball glass with Ginger Ale or Carbonated Water. Add twist of Lemon Peel, if desired, and stir gently.

127

RYE WHISKEY COCKTAIL	1 Dash Bitters 1 Teaspoon Simple Syrup 2 oz. Rye Whiskey Stir well with cracked Ice and strain into 3 oz. Cocktail glass. Serve with a Cherry.
ST. PATRICK'S DAY COCKTAIL	¾ oz. Creme de Menthe (Green) ¾ oz. Green Chartreuse ¾ oz. Irish Whiskey 1 Dash Bitters Stir well with cracked Ice and strain into 3 oz. Cocktail glass.
SALOME COCKTAIL	¾ oz. French Vermouth ¾ oz. Dry Gin ¾ oz. Dubonnet Stir well with cracked Ice and strain into 3 oz. Cocktail glass.
SAN FRANCISCO COCKTAIL	¾ oz. Sloe Gin ¾ oz. Italian Vermouth ¾ oz. French Vermouth 1 Dash Bitters 1 Dash Orange Bitters Shake well with cracked Ice and strain into 3 oz. Cocktail glass. Serve with a Cherry.
SAND-MARTIN COCKTAIL	1 Teaspoon Green Chartreuse 1¼ oz. Italian Vermouth 1¼ oz. Dry Gin Stir well with cracked Ice and strain into 3 oz. Cocktail glass.
SANGAREES	See Index on page 14 for complete list of Sangaree recipes.
SANTIAGO COCKTAIL	½ Teaspoon Powdered Sugar ¼ Teaspoon Grenadine Juice 1 Lime 1½ oz. Imported Rum Shake well with cracked Ice and strain into 3 oz. Cocktail glass.

2 oz. Brandy
2 Dashes Bitters
½ Teaspoon Pineapple Syrup
½ Teaspoon Maraschino
Stir well with cracked Ice and strain
into 3 oz. Cocktail glass.

SARATOGA COCKTAIL

Fill 12 oz. Tom Collins glass with
cracked Ice. Fill with Sarsaparilla.
Insert spiral of Lemon and dangle end
over rim of glass.

SARATOGA COOLER

½ Teaspoon Apricot Flavored Brandy
½ Teaspoon Absinthe Substitute
2 oz. Applejack
Stir well with cracked Ice and strain
into 3 oz. Cocktail glass.

SAUCY SUE COCKTAIL

Use Large Glass Pitcher
4 Teaspoons Powdered Sugar
6 oz. Carbonated Water
½ oz. Triple Sec
½ oz. Curacao
2 oz. Brandy
Fill pitcher with cubes of Ice. Add 1
pint of Sauterne. Stir well and
decorate with as many fruits as
available and also Rind of Cucumber
inserted on each side of pitcher. Top
with small bunch of Mint Sprigs.
Serve in 5 oz. Claret glass.

SAUTERNE CUP

Juice ½ Lime
½ Teaspoon Grenadine
1¾ oz. Imported Rum
1 Twist Orange Peel
Shake well with cracked Ice and strain
into 3 oz. Cocktail glass.

SAXON COCKTAIL

SAZERAC COCKTAIL

Put ¼ Teaspoon Absinthe Substitute into an Old Fashioned Cocktail glass and revolve glass until it is entirely coated with the Absinthe Substitute. Then add:

½ Lump of Sugar
2 Dashes Bitters
  Sufficient water to cover Sugar, and muddle well
2 Cubes of Ice
2 oz. Rye or Bourbon Whiskey

Stir very well. Add Twist of Lemon Peel. (For best results, put glass on Ice for a few minutes before using.)

SCOTCH BISHOP COCKTAIL

1 oz. Scotch Whiskey
½ oz. Orange Juice
½ oz. French Vermouth
½ Teaspoon Triple Sec
¼ Teaspoon Powdered Sugar
  Twist of Lemon Peel

Shake well with cracked Ice and strain into 3 oz. Cocktail glass.

SCOTCH RICKEY

1 Cube of Ice
  Juice ½ Lime
1½ oz. Scotch Whiskey

Fill 8 oz. Highball glass with Carbonated Water and stir. Leave lime in glass.

SCOTCH WHISKEY HIGHBALL

1 Cube of Ice
2 oz. Scotch Whiskey

Fill 8 oz. Highball glass with Ginger Ale or Carbonated Water. Add twist of Lemon Peel, if desired, and stir gently.

Juice ¼ Lemon
1½ oz. Dry Gin
1 Teaspoon Maraschino
3 Sprigs Fresh Mint
Shake well with cracked Ice and strain
into 3 oz. Cocktail glass.

SENSATION COCKTAIL

White of 1 Egg
1½ oz. Rum
Juice ½ Lime
1 Teaspoon Grenadine
Shake well with cracked Ice and strain
into 4 oz. Cocktail glass.

SEPTEMBER MORN COCKTAIL

2 Teaspoons Grapefruit Juice
½ oz. Maraschino
1¼ oz. Dry Gin
Shake well with cracked Ice and strain
into 3 oz. Cocktail glass. Decorate with
Sprig of Fresh Mint.

SEVENTH HEAVEN COCKTAIL

½ Teaspoon Powdered Sugar
1 Egg
1 oz. Port Wine
1 oz. Rum
Shake well with cracked Ice and strain
into 4 oz. Cocktail glass.

SEVILLA COCKTAIL

1½ oz. Irish Whiskey
½ oz. French Vermouth
1 Teaspoon Creme de Menthe
(Green)
Stir well with cracked Ice and strain
into 3 oz. Cocktail glass. Serve with an
Olive.

SHAMROCK COCKTAIL

5 oz. Beer
5 oz. Ginger Ale
Use 12 oz. Tom Collins glass and stir
very gently.

SHANDY GAFF

131

SHANGHAI COCKTAIL

Juice ¼ Lemon
1 Teaspoon Anisette
1 oz. Jamaica Rum
½ Teaspoon Grenadine
Shake well with cracked Ice and strain into 3 oz. Cocktail glass.

SHERRY AND EGG COCKTAIL

Place an egg in a glass, being careful not to break the yolk. Fill glass with sherry. Use 4 oz. Cocktail glass.

SHERRY COBBLER

1 Teaspoon Powdered Sugar
2 oz. Carbonated Water
 Fill 10 oz. Goblet with Shaved Ice
 Add 3 oz. Sherry
Stir well and decorate with fruits in season. Serve with straws.

SHERRY COCKTAIL

2½ oz. Sherry Wine
 1 Dash Bitters
Stir well with cracked Ice and strain into 3 oz. Cocktail glass. Twist of Orange Peel and drop in glass.

SHERRY EGG NOG

1 Egg
1 Teaspoon Powdered Sugar
3 oz. Sherry Wine
 Fill glass with Milk
Shake well with cracked Ice and strain into 12 oz. Tom Collins glass. Grate Nutmeg on top.

SHERRY FLIP

1 Egg
1 Teaspoon Powdered Sugar
1½ oz. Sherry Wine
 2 Teaspoons Sweet Cream
 (if desired)
Shake well with cracked Ice and strain into 5 oz. Flip glass. Grate a little Nutmeg on top.

1 Teaspoon Powdered Sugar
3 oz. Sherry Wine
½ pt. Milk
Shake well with cracked Ice, strain
into 12 oz. Tom Collins glass and grate
Nutmeg on top.

SHERRY MILK PUNCH

1½ oz. Sherry Wine
1 Tablespoon Brandy
1 Teaspoon Powdered Sugar
Shake well with cracked Ice and strain
into 3 oz. Cocktail glass, leaving
enough room in which to float
tablespoon of Port Wine.

SHERRY SANGAREE

1 oz. Sherry Wine
⅓ oz. Brandy
⅓ oz. French Vermouth
⅓ oz. Triple Sec
½ Teaspoon Lemon Juice
Shake well with cracked Ice and strain
into 3 oz. Cocktail glass. Top with
pinch of Cinnamon and twist of Orange
Peel dropped in glass.

SHERRY TWIST COCKTAIL

1¼ oz. Brandy
1¼ oz. Sloe Gin
2 Dashes Bitters
½ Teaspoon Simple Syrup
Stir well with cracked Ice and strain
into 3 oz. Cocktail glass. Twist of
Lemon Peel on top and drop into glass.

SHRINER COCKTAIL

Juice ¼ Lemon
½ oz. Triple Sec
1 oz. Brandy
Shake well with cracked Ice and strain
into 3 oz. Cocktail glass.

SIDECAR COCKTAIL

133

SILVER COCKTAIL

1 oz. French Vermouth
1 oz. Dry Gin
2 Dashes Orange Bitters
¼ Teaspoon Simple Syrup
½ Teaspoon Maraschino
Stir well with cracked Ice and strain into 3 oz. Cocktail glass. Twist of Lemon Peel on top and drop into glass.

SILVER FIZZ

Juice ½ Lemon
1 Teaspoon Powdered Sugar
2 oz. Dry Gin
White of 1 Egg
Shake well with cracked Ice and strain into 8 oz. Highball glass. Fill with Carbonated Water.

**SILVER KING
COCKTAIL**

White of 1 Egg
Juice of ¼ Lemon
1½ oz. Dry Gin
½ Teaspoon Powdered Sugar
2 Dashes Orange Bitters
Shake well with cracked Ice and strain into 4 oz. Cocktail glass.

**SILVER STALLION
FIZZ**

1 Scoop Vanilla Ice Cream
2 oz. Dry Gin
Use 8 oz. Highball glass, stir and fill with Carbonated Water.

**SINGAPORE
SLING**

Juice ½ Lemon
1 Teaspoon Powdered Sugar
2 Cubes of Ice
2 oz. Dry Gin
½ oz. Wild Cherry Flavored Brandy
Serve in 12 oz. Tom Collins glass. Fill with Carbonated Water and stir well. Decorate with fruits in season and serve with straws.

¾ oz. Imported Rum
¾ oz. Brandy
1 Teaspoon Grenadine
1 Teaspoon Curacao
1 Teaspoon Lemon Juice
Shake well with cracked Ice and strain
into 3 oz. Cocktail glass.

SIR WALTER COCKTAIL

¾ oz. Rye or Bourbon Whiskey
¾ oz. French Vermouth
¾ oz. Swedish Punch
1 Dash Bitters
¼ Teaspoon Lemon Juice
Shake well with cracked Ice and
strain into 3 oz. Cocktail glass.

SKYROCKET COCKTAIL

See Index on page 14 for complete list
of Sling recipes.

SLINGS

1 Dash Bitters
2 oz. Sloe Gin
Stir well with cracked Ice and
strain into 3 oz. Cocktail glass.

SLOEBERRY COCKTAIL

2 oz. Sloe Gin
1 Dash Orange Bitters
¼ Teaspoon French Vermouth
Stir well with cracked Ice and strain
into 3 oz. Cocktail glass.

SLOE GIN COCKTAIL

Juice ½ Lemon
1 Teaspoon Powdered Sugar
2 oz. Sloe Gin
Pour into 12 oz. Tom Collins glass. Add
several Cubes of Ice, fill with
Carbonated Water and stir well.
Decorate with slice of Lemon, Orange
and a Cherry. Serve with straws.

SLOE GIN COLLINS

SLOE GIN FIZZ

Juice ½ Lemon
1 Teaspoon Powdered Sugar
2 oz. Sloe Gin
Shake well with cracked Ice and strain into 8 oz. Highball glass. Fill with Carbonated Water. Decorate with slice of Lemon.

SLOE GIN FLIP

1 Egg
1 Teaspoon Powdered Sugar
1 oz. Sloe Gin
½ oz. Apricot Flavored Brandy
2 Teaspoons Sweet Cream
(if desired)
Shake well with cracked Ice and strain into 5 oz. Flip glass. Grate a little Nutmeg on top.

SLOE GIN RICKEY

1 Cube of Ice
Juice of ½ Lime
2 oz. Sloe Gin
Fill 8 oz. Highball glass with Carbonated Water and stir. Leave Lime in glass.

SLOPPY JOE'S COCKTAIL No. 1

Juice 1 Lime
¼ Teaspoon Curacao
¼ Teaspoon Grenadine
¾ oz. Rum
¾ French Vermouth
Shake well with cracked Ice and strain into 3 oz. Cocktail glass.

SLOPPY JOE'S COCKTAIL No. 2

¾ oz. Pineapple Juice
¾ oz. Cognac
¾ oz. Port Wine
¼ Teaspoon Curacao
¼ Teaspoon Grenadine
Shake well with cracked Ice and strain into 3 oz. Cocktail glass.

136

See Index on page 14 for complete list of Smash recipes.

SMASHES

SMILE COCKTAIL

1 oz. Grenadine
1 oz. Dry Gin
½ Teaspoon Lemon Juice
Shake well with cracked Ice and strain into 3 oz. Cocktail glass.

SMILER COCKTAIL

½ oz. Italian Vermouth
½ oz. French Vermouth
1 oz. Dry Gin
1 Dash Bitters
¼ Teaspoon Orange Juice
Shake well with cracked Ice and strain into 3 oz. Cocktail glass.

SNICKER COCKTAIL

¾ oz. French Vermouth
1½ oz. Dry Gin
   White of 1 Egg
½ Teaspoon Maraschino
1 Teaspoon Powdered Sugar
1 Dash Orange Bitters
Shake well with cracked Ice and strain into 4 oz. Cocktail glass.

SNOWBALL COCKTAIL

1½ oz. Dry Gin
½ oz. Anisette
½ oz. Sweet Cream
Shake well with cracked Ice and strain into 4 oz. Cocktail glass.

SOCIETY COCKTAIL

1½ oz. Dry Gin
¾ oz. French Vermouth
¼ Teaspoon Grenadine
Shake well with cracked Ice and strain into 3 oz. Cocktail glass.

SOOTHER COCKTAIL

½ oz. Brandy
½ oz. Applejack
½ oz. Curacao
   Juice ½ Lemon
1 Teaspoon Powdered Sugar
Shake well with cracked Ice and strain into 3 oz. Cocktail glass.

137

SOUL KISS COCKTAIL	¼ oz. Orange Juice ¼ oz. Dubonnet ¾ oz. French Vermouth ¾ oz. Rye or Bourbon Wiskey Shake well with cracked Ice and strain into 3 oz. Cocktail glass.
SOURS	See Index on page 15 for complete list of Sour recipes.
SOUTHERN GIN COCKTAIL	2 oz. Dry Gin 2 Dashes Orange Bitters ½ Teaspoon Curacao Stir well with cracked Ice and strain into 3 oz. Cocktail glass. Twist of Lemon Peel on top and drop into glass.
SOUTH SIDE COCKTAIL	Juice ½ Lemon 1 Teaspoon Powdered Sugar 2 Sprigs Fresh Mint 1½ oz. Dry Gin Shake well with cracked Ice and strain into 3 oz. Cocktail glass.
SOUTH SIDE FIZZ	Juice ½ Lemon 1 Teaspoon Powdered Sugar 2 oz. Dry Gin Shake well with cracked Ice and strain into 7 oz. Highball glass. Fill with Carbonated Water. Add fresh Mint Leaves.
SPANISH TOWN COCKTAIL	2 oz. Rum 1 Teaspoon Curacao Stir well with cracked Ice and strain into 3 oz. Cocktail glass.
SPECIAL ROUGH COCKTAIL	1¼ oz. Applejack 1¼ oz. Brandy ¼ Teaspoon Absinthe Substitute Stir well with cracked Ice and strain into 3 oz. Cocktail glass.

¾ oz. Apricot Flavored Brandy
1½ oz. Dry Gin
1 Dash Bitters
¼ Teaspoon Orange Juice
Shake well with cracked Ice and strain
into 3 oz. Cocktail glass. Add a Cherry
and Twist of Orange Peel on top.

SPENCER COCKTAIL

1½ oz. Dry Gin
¼ oz. Italian Vermouth
¼ oz. French Vermouth
Shake well with cracked Ice and strain
into 3 oz. Cocktail glass. Serve with
Slice of Lemon on top.

SPHINX COCKTAIL

½ oz. Lemon Juice
½ oz. Green Chartreuse
1 oz. Dry Gin
Shake well with cracked Ice and strain
into 3 oz. Cocktail glass.

SPRING FEELING COCKTAIL

Juice ¼ Lemon
1 Teaspoon Grenadine
¾ oz. Dry Gin
¾ oz. Rum
Shake well with cracked Ice and strain
into 3 oz. Cocktail glass.

STANLEY COCKTAIL

1 oz. Applejack
1 oz. Italian Vermouth
1 Dash Bitters
Stir well with cracked Ice and strain
into 3 oz. Cocktail glass. Twist of
Lemon Peel on top and drop into glass.

STAR COCKTAIL

STAR DAISY

Juice ½ Lemon
½ Teaspoon Powdered Sugar
1 Teaspoon Raspberry Syrup or Grenadine
1 oz. Dry Gin
1 oz. Applejack
Shake well with cracked Ice and strain into Stein or 8 oz. Metal Cup. Add Cube of Ice and decorate with Fruit.

STARS AND STRIPES POUSSE CAFE

⅓ Grenadine
⅓ Creme de Menthe (White)
⅓ Creme de Yvette
Pour carefully, in order given, into Pousse Cafe glass, so that each ingredient floats on preceding one.

STINGER COCKTAIL

1 oz. Creme de Menthe (White)
1 oz. Brandy
Shake well with cracked Ice and strain into 3 oz. Cocktail glass.

STONE COCKTAIL

½ oz. Imported Rum
½ oz. Italian Vermouth
1 oz. Sherry Wine
Shake well with cracked Ice and strain into 3 oz. Cocktail glass.

STONE FENCE HIGHBALL

1 Cube of Ice
2 Dashes Bitters
2 oz. Scotch Whiskey
Use 8 oz. Highball glass and fill with Carbonated Water, and stir gently.

¾ oz. Dry Gin
1½ oz. Sherry Wine
Stir well with cracked Ice and strain
into 3 oz. Cocktail glass.

**STRAIGHT LAW
COCKTAIL**

1½ oz. Absinthe Substitute
½ oz. Anisette
White of 1 Egg
Shake well with cracked Ice and strain
into 4 oz. Cocktail glass.

**SUISSESSE
COCKTAIL**

¾ oz. Italian Vermouth
1½ oz. Dry Gin
1 Dash Bitters
Stir well with cracked Ice and strain
into 3 oz. Cocktail glass. Twist of
Orange Peel on top and drop into
glass.

**SUNSHINE
COCKTAIL**

Juice ½ Lime
2 Cubes of Ice
2 oz. Imported Rum
Fill 12 oz. Tom Collins glass with
Ginger Ale and stir gently.

SUSIE TAYLOR

½ Teaspoon Absinthe Substitute
2 Dashes Bitters
¾ oz. French Vermouth
1½ oz. Rye or Bourbon Whiskey
Shake well with cracked Ice and strain
into 3 oz. Cocktail glass.

**SWISS FAMILY
COCKTAIL**

See Index on page 15 for complete list
of Swizzle recipes.

SWIZZLES

¾ oz. Dry Gin
¾ oz. Italian Vermouth
¾ oz. Green Chartreuse
1 Dash Orange Bitters
Stir well with cracked Ice and strain
into 3 oz. Cocktail glass. Twist of
Lemon Peel on top and serve with
Cherry or Olive.

**TAILSPIN
COCKTAIL**

TANGO COCKTAIL

½ oz. Orange Juice
½ oz. French Vermouth
½ oz. Italian Vermouth
1 oz. Dry Gin
½ Teaspoon Curacao
Shake well with cracked Ice and strain into 4 oz. Cocktail glass.

TEMPTATION COCKTAIL

1½ oz. Rye or Bourbon Whiskey
½ Teaspoon Curacao
½ Teaspoon Absinthe Substitute
½ Teaspoon Dubonnet
1 Twist Orange Peel
1 Twist Lemon Peel
Shake well with cracked Ice and strain into 3 oz. Cocktail glass.

TEMPTER COCKTAIL

1 oz. Port Wine
1 oz. Apricot Flavored Brandy
Shake well with cracked Ice and strain into 3 oz. Cocktail glass.

THANKSGIVING SPECIAL COCKTAIL

¾ oz. Apricot Nectar Liqueur
¾ oz. Dry Gin
¾ oz. French Vermouth
¼ Teaspoon Lemon Juice
Shake well with cracked Ice and strain into 3 oz. Cocktail glass. Serve with a Cherry.

THIRD DEGREE COCKTAIL

1½ oz. Dry Gin
¾ oz. French Vermouth
1 Teaspoon Absinthe Substitute
Stir well with cracked Ice and strain into 3 oz. Cocktail glass.

¾ oz. Imported Rum
¾ oz. Applejack
¾ oz. Brandy
¼ Teaspoon Absinthe Substitute
Stir well with cracked Ice and strain
into 3 oz. Cocktail glass.

1¼ oz. Italian Vermouth
1¼ oz. Scotch Whiskey
 2 Dashes Bitters
Stir well with cracked Ice and strain
into 3 oz. Cocktail glass.

THISTLE COCKTAIL

1¼ oz. Imported Rum
 ¾ oz. Brandy
 1 Teaspoon Grenadine
 ¼ Teaspoon Lemon Juice
Shake well with cracked Ice and strain
into 3 oz. Cocktail glass.

THREE MILLER COCKTAIL

1 oz. Dry Gin
½ oz. French Vermouth
½ oz. Orange Juice
Shake well with cracked Ice and strain
into 3 oz. Cocktail glass.

THREE STRIPES COCKTAIL

1 Teaspoon Powdered Sugar
 Yolk of 1 Egg
1½ oz. Brandy
 1 Pinch of Cayenne Pepper
Shake well with cracked Ice and strain
into 4 oz. Cocktail glass.

THUNDER COCKTAIL

 Yolk of 1 Egg
 1 Teaspoon Powdered Sugar
1½ oz. Brandy
Shake well with cracked Ice and strain
into 4 oz. Cocktail glass.

THUNDER AND LIGHTNING COCKTAIL

THUNDERCLAP COCKTAIL	¾ oz. Dry Gin
	¾ oz. Rye or Bourbon Whiskey
	¾ oz. Brandy
	Stir well with cracked Ice and strain into 3 oz. Cocktail glass.

TIPPERARY COCKTAIL	¾ oz. Irish Whiskey
	¾ oz. Green Chartreuse
	¾ oz. Italian Vermouth
	Stir well with cracked Ice and strain into 3 oz. Cocktail glass.

T. N. T. COCKTAIL	1¼ oz. Rye or Bourbon Whiskey
	1¼ oz. Absinthe Substitute
	Stir well with cracked Ice and strain into 3 oz. Cocktail glass.

TODDIES	See Index on page 15 for complete list of Toddy recipes.

TOM AND JERRY

First prepare batter, using mixing bowl. Separate the yolk and white of 1 Egg, beating each separately and thoroughly. Then combine both, adding enough superfine Powdered Sugar to stiffen. Add to this 1 pinch of Baking Soda and ¼ oz. Imported Rum to preserve the batter. Then add a little more Sugar to stiffen.

To serve, use hot Tom and Jerry mug, using 1 tablespoon of above batter, dissolved in 3 tablespoons Hot Milk. Add 1½ oz. Imported Rum. Then fill mug with Hot Milk within ¼ inch of top of mug and stir gently. Then top with ½ oz. Brandy and grate a little Nutmeg on top.

The secret of a Tom and Jerry is to have a stiff batter and a warm mug.

Juice ½ Lemon
1 Teaspoon Powdered Sugar
2 oz. Dry Gin
Pour into 12 oz. Tom Collins glass. Add
several cubes of Ice, fill with
Carbonated Water and stir well.
Decorate with slice of Lemon, Orange
and a Cherry. Serve with straws.

TOM COLLINS

1½ oz. Rye or Bourbon Whiskey
¾ oz. Italian Vermouth
2 Dashes Orange Bitters
Shake well with cracked Ice and strain
into 3 oz. Cocktail glass.

TRILBY COCKTAIL

¾ oz. Italian Vermouth
¾ oz. French Vermouth
¾ oz. Dry Gin
Stir well with cracked Ice and strain
into 3 oz. Cocktail glass.

**TRINITY
COCKTAIL**

¾ oz. Creme de Cacao
¾ oz. Maraschino
¾ oz. French Vermouth
1 Dash Bitters
Stir well with cracked Ice and strain
into 3 oz. Cocktail glass.

**TROPICAL
COCKTAIL**

¼ oz. Lemon Juice
¼ oz. Apricot Flavored Brandy
¾ oz. Italian Vermouth
¾ oz. Apple Brandy
Shake well with cracked Ice and strain
into 3 oz. Cocktail glass.

TULIP COCKTAIL

¼ Teaspoon Absinthe Substitute
2 Dashes Bitters
1 oz. French Vermouth
1 oz. Dry Gin
Stir well with cracked Ice and strain
into 3 oz. Cocktail glass. Twist of
Orange Peel and drop in glass.

TURF COCKTAIL

TUXEDO	1¼ oz. Dry Gin
COCKTAIL	1¼ oz. French Vermouth
	¼ Teaspoon Maraschino
	¼ Teaspoon Absinthe Substitute
	2 Dashes Orange Bitters

Stir well with cracked Ice and strain into 3 oz. Cocktail glass. Serve with a Cherry.

TWIN SIX	1 oz. Dry Gin
COCKTAIL	½ oz. Italian Vermouth
	¼ Teaspoon Grenadine
	½ oz. Orange Juice
	White of 1 Egg

Shake well with cracked Ice and strain into 4 oz. Cocktail glass.

ULANDA	1½ oz. Dry Gin
COCKTAIL	¾ oz. Triple Sec
	¼ Teaspoon Absinthe

Stir well with cracked Ice and strain into 3 oz. Cocktail glass.

UNION JACK	¾ oz. Creme de Yvette
COCKTAIL	1½ oz. Dry Gin
	½ Teaspoon Grenadine

Shake well with cracked Ice and strain into 3 oz. Cocktail glass.

VALENCIA	½ oz. Orange Juice
COCKTAIL	1½ oz. Apricot Flavored Brandy
	2 Dashes Orange Bitters

Shake well with cracked Ice and strain into 3 oz. Cocktail glass.

VANDERBILT	¾ oz. Wild Cherry Flavored Brandy
COCKTAIL	1½ oz. Brandy
	1 Teaspoon Simple Syrup
	2 Dashes Bitters

Stir well with cracked Ice and strain into 3 oz. Cocktail glass.

1½ oz. Dry Gin
¾ oz. Rhubarb Syrup
Shake well with cracked Ice and strain
into 3 oz. Cocktail glass. Serve with
Sprig of Fresh Mint.

VEGETARIAN GIN COCKTAIL

¾ oz. Creme de Cassis
1½ oz. French Vermouth
1 Cube of Ice
Fill 8 oz. Highball glass with
Carbonated Water and stir.

VERMOUTH CASSIS

1 oz. French Vermouth
1 oz. Italian Vermouth
1 Dash Orange Bitters
Stir well with cracked Ice and strain
into 3 oz. Cocktail glass. Serve with a
Cherry.

VERMOUTH COCKTAIL

½ oz. Dry Gin
1¼ oz. Italian Vermouth
½ oz. Brandy
Stir well with cracked Ice and strain
into 3 oz. Cocktail glass.

VICTOR COCKTAIL

Juice ½ Lemon
½ Teaspoon Powdered Sugar
1½ oz. Dry Gin
½ oz. Creme de Yvette
Shake well with cracked Ice and strain
into 7 oz. Highball glass. Fill with
Carbonated Water.

VIOLET FIZZ

1¼ oz. French Vermouth
1¼ oz. Dry Gin
1 Teaspoon Curacao
Stir well with cracked Ice and strain
into 3 oz. Cocktail glass

WALLICK COCKTAIL

WARDAY'S COCKTAIL

¾ oz. Italian Vermouth
¾ oz. Dry Gn
¾ oz. Apple Brandy
1 Teaspoon Chartreuse
Stir well with cracked Ice and strain into 3 oz. Cocktail glass.

WARD EIGHT

Juice ½ Lemon
1 Teaspoon Powdered Sugar
1 Teaspoon Grenadine
2 oz. Rye or Bourbon Whiskey
Shake well with cracked Ice and strain into 8 oz. Stem glass previously prepared with 2 cubes of Ice, slice of Orange, Lemon and a Cherry. Serve with straws.

WASHINGTON COCKTAIL

1½ oz. French Vermouth
¾ oz. Brandy
2 Dashes Bitters
½ Teaspoon Simple Syrup
Stir well with cracked Ice and strain into 3 oz. Cocktail glass.

WATERBURY COCKTAIL

½ Teaspoon Powdered Sugar
Juice ¼ Lemon or ½ Lime
White of 1 Egg
1½ oz. Brandy
½ Teaspoon Grenadine
Shake well with cracked Ice and strain into 4 oz. Cocktail glass.

WEBSTER COCKTAIL

Juice ½ Lime
¼ oz. Apricot Flavored Brandy
½ oz. French Vermouth
1 oz. Dry Gin
Shake well with cracked Ice and strain into 3 oz. Cocktail glass.

¼ oz. Orange Juice
¼ oz. Wild Cherry Flavored Brandy
¾ oz. Dry Gin
¾ oz. Dubonnet
Shake well with cracked Ice and strain
into 3 oz. Cocktail glass.

WEDDING BELLE COCKTAIL

Juice ½ Lime
¾ oz. Dubonnet
¾ oz. Brandy
¼ Teaspoon Maraschino
Shake well with cracked Ice and strain
into 3 oz. Cocktail glass.

WEEP NO MORE COCKTAIL

¾ oz. French Vermouth
1½ oz. Dry Gin
¼ Teaspoon Apricot Flavored
    Brandy
½ Teaspoon Apple Brandy
Stir well with cracked Ice and strain
into 3 oz. cocktail glass.

WEMBLEY COCKTAIL

Juice 1 Lime
1 Teaspoon Powdered Sugar
2 oz. Rum
Agitate in electric mixer filled with
shaved Ice for about 2 minutes. Strain
through coarse meshed strainer into 6
oz. Champagne glass.

WEST INDIES FROSTED COCKTAIL

½ oz. Apricot Flavored Brandy
1 oz. Dry Gin
½ oz. French Vermouth
¼ Teaspoon Lemon Juice
Shake well with cracked Ice and strain
into 3 oz. Cocktail glass.

WESTERN ROSE COCKTAIL

WHIP COCKTAIL

½ oz. French Vermouth
½ oz. Italian Vermouth
1¼ oz. Brandy
¼ Teaspoon Absinthe Substitute
1 Teaspoon Curacao
Stir well with cracked Ice and strain into 3 oz. Cocktail glass.

**WHISKEY
COBBLER**

1 Teaspoon Powdered Sugar
2 oz. Carbonated Water
  Fill 10 oz. Goblet with Shaved Ice
  Add 2 oz. Rye or Bourbon Whiskey
Stir well and decorate with fruits in season. Serve with straws.

**WHISKEY
COCKTAIL**

1 Dash Bitters
1 Teaspoon Simple Syrup
2 oz. Rye or Bourbon Whiskey
Stir well with cracked Ice and strain into 3 oz. Cocktail glass. Serve with a Cherry.

**WHISKEY
COLLINS**

Juice ½ Lemon
1 Teaspoon Powdered Sugar
2 oz. Rye or Burbon Whiskey
Pour into 12 oz. Tom Collins glass. Add several cubes of Ice, fill with Carbonated Water and stir well. Decorate with slice of Lemon, Orange and a Cherry. Serve with straws.

WHISKEY DAISY

Juice of ½ Lemon
½ Teaspoon Powdered Sugar
1 Teaspoon Raspberry Syrup or Grenadine
2 oz. Rye or Bourbon Whiskey
Shake well with cracked Ice and strain into Stein or 8 oz. Metal cup. Add cube of Ice and decorate with fruit.

1 Egg
1 Teaspoon Powdered Sugar
2 oz. Rye or Bourbon Whiskey
  Fill glass with Milk
Shake well with cracked Ice and strain
into 12 oz. Tom Collins glass. Grate
Nutmeg on top.

WHISKEY EGG NOGG

  Juice ½ Lemon
1 Teaspoon Powdered Sugar
1 Teaspoon Water and stir
  Fill glass with Shaved Ice
2½ oz. Rye or Bourbon Whiskey
Use 12 oz. Tom Collins glass. Stir well.
Add slice of Lemon. Serve with
straws.

WHISKEY FIX

1 Egg
1 Teaspoon Powdered Sugar
1½ oz. Rye or Bourbon Whiskey
2 Teaspoons Sweet Cream
  (if desired)
Shake well with cracked Ice and strain
into 5 oz. Flip glass. Grate a little
Nutmeg on top.

WHISKEY FLIP

1 Cube of Ice
2 oz. Rye or Bourbon Whiskey
Fill 8 oz. Highball glass with Ginger
Ale or Carbonated Water. Add twist
of Lemon Peel, if desired, and stir
gently.

WHISKEY HIGHBALL

1 Teaspoon Powdered Sugar
2 oz. Rye or Bourbon Whiskey
½ pt. Milk
Shake well with cracked Ice, strain
into 12 oz. Tom Collins glass and grate
Nutmeg on top.

WHISKEY MILK PUNCH

151

WHISKEY ORANGE	Juice ½ Orange 1 Teaspoon Powdered Sugar ½ Teaspoon Absinthe Substitute 1½ oz. Rye or Bourbon Whiskey Shake well with cracked Ice and strain into 8 oz. Highball glass. Decorate with Slice of Orange and Lemon.
WHISKEY RICKEY	1 Cube of Ice Juice of ½ Lime 1½ oz. Rye or Bourbon Whiskey Fill 8 oz. Highball glass with Carbonated Water and stir. Leave Lime in glass.
WHISKEY SANGAREE	1½ oz. Rye or Bourbon Whiskey 1 Teaspoon Powdered Sugar Shake well with cracked Ice and strain into 3 oz. Cocktail glass, leaving enough room in which to float a tablespoon of Port Wine.
WHISKEY SKIN	Put Lump of Sugar into Hot Whiskey glass and fill with two-thirds Boiling Water. Add 2 oz. Rye or Bourbon Whiskey. Stir, then add Twist of Lemon Peel on top and drop in glass.
WHISKEY SLING	Dissolve 1 Teaspoon Powdered Sugar in Teaspoon of Water 2 oz. Rye or Bourbon Whiskey 2 Cubes of Ice Serve in Old Fashioned Cocktail glass and stir. Twist of Lemon Peel on top and drop in glass.

152

Muddle 1 Lump of Sugar with
1 oz. Carbonated Water and
4 Sprigs of Green Mint
  Add 2 oz. Rye or Bourbon Whiskey,
  Then a Cube of Ice
Stir and decorate with a slice of
Orange and a Cherry. Twist Lemon
Peel on top. Use Old Fashioned
Cocktail glass.

**WHISKEY
SMASH**

Juice ½ Lemon
½ Teaspoon Powdered Sugar
2 oz. Rye or Bourbon Whiskey
Shake well with cracked Ice and strain
into 6 oz. Sour glass. Fill with
Carbonated Water. Decorate with a
half-slice of Lemon and a Cherry.

WHISKEY SOUR

1½ oz. Rye or Bourbon Whiskey
1 Tablespoon Powdered Sugar
1 Tablespoon Raspberry Syrup or
  Grenadine
Stir well with cracked Ice and strain
into 8 oz. Highball glass and fill with
Carbonated Water. Decorate with
cubes of Pineapple and Strawberries.

WHISKEY SQUIRT

Made same as Gin Swizzle, using 2 oz.
Rye or Bourbon Whiskey.

**WHISKEY
SWIZZLE**

Use Old Fashioned Cocktail glass.
½ Teaspoon Powdered Sugar
2 Teaspoons Water
2 oz. Rye or Bourbon Whiskey
1 Lump of Ice
Stir well and twist Lemon Peel on top.

WHISKEY TODDY

153

WHISKEY TODDY
[Hot]

Put Lump of Sugar into Hot Whiskey glass and fill with two-thirds Boiling Water. Add 2 oz. Rye or Bourbon Whiskey. Stir and decorate with slice of Lemon. Grate Nutmeg on top.

WHISPERS OF THE FROST COCKTAIL

¾ oz. Rye or Bourbon Whiskey
¾ oz. Sherry Wine
¾ oz. Port Wine
1 Teaspoon Powdered Sugar
Shake well with cracked Ice and strain into 3 oz. Cocktail glass. Serve with Slices of Lemon and Orange.

WHITE CARGO COCKTAIL

1 Small Scoop Vanilla Ice Cream
1 oz. Dry Gin
Shake until thoroughly mixed and add Water or Sauterne if the mixture is too thick. Serve in 4 oz. Cocktail glass.

WHITE LADY COCKTAIL

White of 1 Egg
1 Teaspoon Powdered Sugar
1 Teaspoon Sweet Cream
1½ oz. Dry Gin
Shake well with cracked Ice and strain into 4 oz. Cocktail glass.

WHITE LILY COCKTAIL

¾ oz. Triple Sec
¾ oz. Rum
¾ oz. Dry Gin
¼ Teaspoon Anisette
Shake well with cracked Ice and strain into 3 oz. Cocktail glass.

Juice ½ Lemon
1 Teaspoon Powdered Sugar
2 Dashes Bitters
½ Teaspoon Grenadine
1½ oz. Imported Rum
Shake well with cracked Ice and strain
into 3 oz. Cocktail glass.

**WHITE LION
COCKTAIL**

Pour 2 oz. Rye or Bourbon Whiskey
into Delmonico glass. Fill balance with
Milk and drink without stirring.

WHITE PLUSH

¾ oz. Dry Gin
½ oz. Orange Juice
Juice 1 Lime
½ oz. Maraschino
White of 1 Egg
Shake well with cracked Ice and strain
into 4 oz. Cocktail glass.

**WHITE ROSE
COCKTAIL**

¾ oz. Creme de Menthe (White)
1½ oz. Dry Gin
Shake well with cracked Ice and strain
into 3 oz. Cocktail glass.

**WHITE WAY
COCKTAIL**

1½ oz. Benedictine
1 Whole Egg
Shake well with cracked Ice and strain
into 4 oz. Cocktail glass. Float 1
teaspoon of Cream on top.

**WIDOW'S DREAM
COCKTAIL**

½ oz. Yellow Chartreuse
½ oz. Benedictine
1 oz. Apple Brandy
1 Dash Bitters
Shake well with cracked Ice and strain
into 3 oz. Cocktail glass. Strawberry
may be served on top.

**WIDOW'S KISS
COCKTAIL**

WILD EYED ROSE HIGHBALL	Juice of ½ Lime ½ oz. Grenadine 2 oz. Irish Whiskey 1 Cube of Ice Fill 8 oz. Highball glass with Carbonated Water and stir gently.
WINDY CORNER COCKTAIL	2 oz. Blackberry Flavored Brandy Stir well with cracked Ice and strain into 3 oz. Cocktail glass. Grate a little Nutmeg on top.
XANTHIA COCKTAIL	¾ oz. Wild Cherry Flavored Brandy ¾ oz. Yellow Chartreuse ¾ oz. Dry Gin Stir well with cracked Ice and strain into 3 oz. Cocktail glass.
XERES COCKTAIL	1 Dash Orange Bitters 2 oz. Sherry Wine Stir well with cracked Ice and strain into 3 oz. Cocktail glass.
X. Y. Z. COCKTAIL	½ oz. Lemon Juice ½ oz. Triple Sec 1 oz. Rum Shake well with cracked Ice and strain into 3 oz. Cocktail glass.
YALE COCKTAIL	1½ oz. Dry Gin ½ oz. French Vermouth 1 Dash Bitters 1 Teaspoon Creme de Yvette Shake well with cracked Ice and strain into 3 oz. Cocktail glass.

YELLOW PARROT COCKTAIL

¾ oz. Anisette
¾ oz. Yellow Chartreuse
¾ oz. Apricot Flavored Brandy
Stir well with cracked Ice and strain
into 3 oz. Cocktail glass.

ZANZIBAR COCKTAIL

¾ oz. Lemon Juice
¾ oz. Dry Gin
¾ oz. French Vermouth
¼ Teaspoon Powdered Sugar
1 Dash Orange Bitters
Shake well with cracked Ice and strain
into 3 oz. Cocktail glass. Serve with
slice of Lemon.

ZAZA COCKTAIL

1½ oz. Dry Gin
¾ oz. Dubonnet
1 Twist Oange Peel
Stir well with cracked Ice and strain
into 3 oz. Cocktail glass.

ZOMBIE

1 oz. Passion Fruit Juice
1 oz. Plum or Apricot Juice
    Juice 1 small Lime—drop in skin
1 Teaspoon Powdered Sugar
1 Dash Bitters
    Juice 1 medium-small Orange
½ oz. Anisette
2½ oz. Rum
½ oz. Apricot Flavored Brandy
⅔ oz. Demerara Rum, 151 proof
1 oz. Jamaica Rum
1 oz. Porto Rican Gold Label Rum
Add cracked Ice and agitate for full
minute in Electric Mixing Machine (If
none available, shake very well in
Cocktail Shaker), and strain into 14 oz.
Frosted Zombie glass. Decorate with
¼" square of Pineapple and 1 Green
and 1 Red Cherry, also sprig of Fresh
Mint dipped in Powdered Sugar.
Serve with straws.

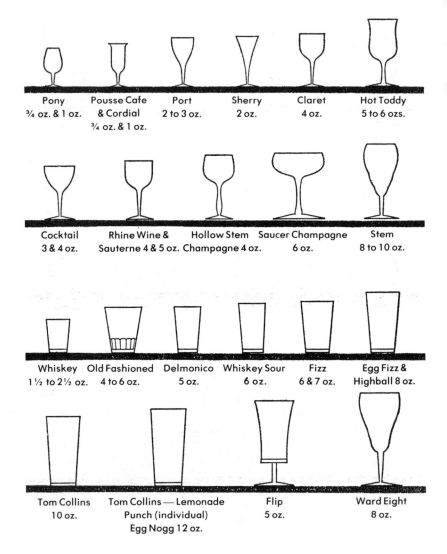

Pony
¾ oz. & 1 oz.

Pousse Cafe
& Cordial
¾ oz. & 1 oz.

Port
2 to 3 oz.

Sherry
2 oz.

Claret
4 oz.

Hot Toddy
5 to 6 ozs.

Cocktail
3 & 4 oz.

Rhine Wine &
Sauterne 4 & 5 oz.

Hollow Stem
Champagne 4 oz.

Saucer Champagne
6 oz.

Stem
8 to 10 oz.

Whiskey
1 ½ to 2 ½ oz.

Old Fashioned
4 to 6 oz.

Delmonico
5 oz.

Whiskey Sour
6 oz.

Fizz
6 & 7 oz.

Egg Fizz &
Highball 8 oz.

Tom Collins
10 oz.

Tom Collins — Lemonade
Punch (individual)
Egg Nogg 12 oz.

Flip
5 oz.

Ward Eight
8 oz.

158

Balloon Shape Beer Goblet

Beer Goblet 8 to 10 oz.

Pilsner Glass Porter Ale 8 to 14 oz.

Brandy Inhaler

Bitter Bottle

Punch Bowl & Cup

Beer Stein-10 oz.

Combination Shaker

Shaker & Mixing Glass

Tom & Jerry Bowl & Mug

Strainer

Muddler

159

WHEN TO SERVE BEVERAGES

APPETIZER	Cocktails, Dry Sherry or Madeira
HORS-d'OEUVRES	Moselle or White Burgundy
OYSTERS	
SOUP	Sherry or Dry Madeira
FISH	Rhine Wine, Moselle or White Burgundy
ENTREE	Light Red wines of Bordeaux or Burgundy
ROAST	Champagne
GAME	Burgundy
DESSERT	Sweet Madeira, Tokay or Muscatel
CHEESE	Port
FRUIT	White Port, Malaga or Tokay
COFFEE	Cordial

Care should be taken never to follow a sweet wine by a dry wine or a heavy wine by a light wine.

Champagne is the only wine that may be served with any course and at all times during the meal.

* * * * *

RECIPE FOR SIMPLE SYRUP

Stir 1 lb. Granulated Sugar into 1 Pint of Boiling Water. Continue to boil for about 5 minutes. Then cool and bottle. Store in a cool place.

* * * * *

Because of the fact that sugar is not easily dissolved in alcohol it is best, especially in drinks that are to be stirred rather than shaken, to dissolve the sugar before adding the liquor.